New Library of Pastoral Care
GENERAL EDITOR: DEREK BLOWS

Being Your Age

New Library of Pastoral Care

NEW·LIBRARY·OF

PASTORAL·CARE

BEING YOUR AGE

Pastoral Care for Older People

Michael Butler
and
Ann Orbach

SPCK

First published in Great Britain 1993
Society for Promoting Christian Knowledge
Holy Trinity Church
Marylebone Road
London NW1 4DU

The publishers are grateful to Faber and Faber Ltd for permission
to reproduce extracts from Four Quartets by T. S. Eliot,
published in 1942.

British Library Cataloguing-in-Publication Data

A catalogue record for this book is available from the British Library

ISBN 0-281-04646-8

Typeset by Pioneer Associates, Perthshire
Printed in Great Britain by
The Cromwell Press Melksham, Wiltshire

Contents

Foreword

The *New Library of Pastoral Care* has been planned to meet
the needs of those people concerned with pastoral care,
whether clergy or lay, who seek to improve their knowledge
and skills in this field. Equally, it is hoped that it may prove
useful to those secular helpers who may wish to understand
the role of the pastor.

Pastoral care in every age has drawn from contemporary
secular knowledge to inform its understanding of men and
women and their various needs and of the ways in which
these needs might be met. Today it is perhaps the secular
helping professions of social work, counselling and psychotherapy, and community development which have particular
contributions to make to pastors in their work. Such
knowledge does not stand still, and pastors would have a
struggle to keep up with the endless tide of new developments
which pour out from these and other disciplines, and to sort
out which ideas and practices might be relevant to their
particular pastoral needs. Among present-day ideas, for
instance, of particular value might be an understanding of
the social context of the pastoral task, the dynamics of the
helping relationship, the attitudes and skills as well as factual
knowledge which might make for effective pastoral inter-
vention and, perhaps most significant of all, the study of
particular cases, whether through verbatim reports of inter-
views or general case presentation. The discovery of ways of
learning from what one is doing is becoming increasingly
important.

There is always a danger that a pastor who drinks deeply
at the well of a secular discipline may risk losing a distinct
pastoral identity and become 'just another' social worker or
counsellor. It in no way detracts from the value of these
professions to assert that the role and task of the pastor are
quite unique among the helping professions and deserve to be

clarified and strengthened rather than weakened. The theological commitment of the pastors and the appropriate use of their role will be a recurrent theme of the series. At the same time pastors cannot afford to work in a vacuum. They need to be able to communicate and co-operate with those helpers in other disciplines whose work may overlap, without loss of their own unique status. This in turn will mean being able to communicate with them through some understanding of their concepts and language.

Finally, there is a rich variety of styles and approaches in pastoral work within the various religious traditions. No attempt will be made to secure a uniform approach. The Library will contain the variety, and even perhaps occasional eccentricity, which such a title suggests. Some books will be more specifically theological and others more concerned with particular areas of need or practice. It is hoped that all of them will have a usefulness that will reach right across the boundaries of religious denomination.

DEREK BLOWS
Series Editor

Preface

The phrase 'pastoral care' has been borrowed by a secular world from the Christian Church. As such, it is thoroughly biblical in origin. Every Christian minister is reminded at his ordination that he preaches, teaches, cares for and administers his 'flock' only in the name of Christ, the supreme 'Pastor' and 'Good Shepherd', as symbolized in the bishop's 'pastoral staff'.

In the contemporary world the word 'pastoral' has a wider usage, and this book is intended not only for clergy, but also for social workers, counsellors, therapists, and all those, whether professional or not, who undertake the care of people older than themselves. To the young and active, this can seem a daunting task: one that takes them into an 'undiscovered country' that is still distant and out of sight. But ageing is not a condition belonging only to the future. It happens to all of us and begins as soon as we are born. With the threat of AIDS and a high incidence of cancer among the relatively young, some of us have had to speed up our ageing and to face experiences, both of bereavement and our own dying, that we had hoped to postpone to a much later decade. In contrast, a great many others are living far longer than their original expectations.

Thus this book is addressed to all of us: the old and those who have yet to face growing old, the carers, and those for whom they care. We must never forget that *people* matter and matter supremely. They need to be respected and they need to be listened to.

To quote from a book written fifty years ago: 'It is through our response to other persons that we become persons . . . *All real life is meeting*' (J. H. Oldham. *Real Life is Meeting*, SCM 1942).

MICHAEL BUTLER
ANN ORBACH
May 1992

ix

Acknowledgements

We would like to thank the Rev. John James and his wife, Valerie, for constructive criticism and additional material; Mona Schaanning, for her help in checking the index; Peter Ardern of St James's Hospital, Portsmouth, for his information on those who care for Alzheimer sufferers; the Rev. Keith Nevel, for giving us a Canadian perspective on care for older people; and the help and co-operation of the numerous religious communities who responded to our questions. We would also like to acknowledge those many people, both named and anonymous, who allowed us to visit, interview, quote and write about them.

Part I

The Phenomenon of Ageing

ONE

Images of Ageing

White hair: relegation.
Instant dismissal. Just one of those oldies.
Past action or thought.

White hair: anonymity.
Faceless old nuisance to put into care.
One more for the file.

But white hair is freedom.
Release from convention. At last unrestricted.
To act as you please.

Yes, white hair's a distinction.
It shines in the sunshine like snowfall in winter,
A badge of experience.
One who survives.

Jean Thompson

The writer of these verses is realistic. She sees the
depressingly negative image, but her own positive self-esteem
triumphs. However, old people need to be extra strong to
survive such negativity. Probably few of us realize how
powerfully the popular image of 'an old bag' affects the way
our senior citizens get treated. Let us begin, therefore, with a
rather surprising story.

For some thousand hours, over a three-year period, an
American called Pat Moore disguised herself as an old woman.
She went out in public to test whether there was evidence of
discrimination against the elderly. She proved her point, for
she experienced considerable discrimination. She was mocked,
abused and assaulted. She received little or no help in shops,

3

queues and on public transport. At a later date, an English student nurse called Sheila Green attempted to replicate Pat Moore's research by repeating the experiment in Britain. With the help of a professional make-up artist and suitable clothes, together with a walking stick, she disguised herself as an old woman. She then set herself various tasks. These included examining cosmetics at a beauty counter, struggling to get on a crowded 'pay-as-you-enter' bus, going through a supermarket checkout, waiting at a hospital out-patients' department and buying fruit and vegetables in a street market. First, though, she made certain preparations:

> As I practised walking round the house, I realised how difficult it would be to maintain an elderly person's stoop and gait, so I made a brace from an apron and a crepe bandage, which prevented me from standing erect. I also wrapped adhesive tape round my feet to make me more inclined to shuffle, and wrapped tape round my fingers to simulate arthritis.
>
> With gloves on, plugs in my ears to dull my hearing and drops in my eyes to impair my vision, I was ready to start my experiment.[1]

In summing up her response to the way she was treated, she wrote: 'I felt alone, isolated and, at times, threatened and frightened. Most of all I was angry, angry that people do not notice other people's pain, anxiety and helplessness, and realise that they need help and patience rather than abuse.'[2]

Sheila Green became very aware, through lack of hearing, how much non-verbal language is used, and how upsetting it is not to be able to pick up the symbols given in daily contact between people. Also, she realized what it is like to be ignored. 'She's a bad-tempered old begger' took on a whole new meaning.

The irony of Sheila Green's experiment was that she returned to the same stores, market and bus queues, but this time as her normal self. She made the same mistakes, fumbled for coins and prodded fruit on the stalls, but met with no abuse. She came to the conclusion that if people were feeling irritable or having a bad day, they felt safe taking it out on an elderly person — someone who was unlikely to have the strength to hit back.

Where do these negative images of ageing originate? After all, ageing is a normal process that begins from the moment of conception. 'Growing up' and 'coming of age' are welcome landmarks for young people, and can be seen as part of their rites of passage. But the phrases 'Act your age' or 'What do you expect at your age?' are terms of rebuke.

A letter to the *Observer* (3 October 1989) refers to previous correspondence on the use of the word 'wrinklies': 'Surely our first aim should be the abolition of the use of this adjective as a noun. "Wrinkly", when used to designate an old person, is not amusing; it is semantically incorrect, rude and unkind. After all, we, old people, do not describe our teenage friends as "the spotties".'

The term 'ageism' was coined in 1968 by the American psychiatrist, Robert Butler. His Pulitzer prize-winning *Why Survive?*, published in 1975, did much to popularize the notion. According to Butler, ageism is a deep prejudice against the elderly, manifested in stereotypes, myths, disdain and dislike, as well as in a subtle avoidance of contact. It also includes discriminating practices in housing, employment and services of all kinds, not to mention epithets, cartoons and jobs.

Alex Comfort trenchantly describes ageism as 'the notion that people cease to be people, cease to be the same people or become people of a distant and inferior kind, by virtue of having lived a specified number of years'. He devises a profile of a member of this so-called 'inferior race':

> He or she is white-haired, inactive, unemployed, making no demands on anyone, docile in putting up with loneliness, rip-offs of every kind and boredom, and able to live on a pittance. He or she . . . is slightly deficient in intellect, and tiresome to talk to . . . asexual, because old people are incapable of sexual activity, and it is unseemly if they are not. He or she is unemployable because old age is second childhood and everyone knows that the old make a mess of simple work. Some credit points can be gained by meeting or being nice to these subhuman individuals, but most of

them prefer their own company and the company of other aged unfortunates. Their main occupations are religion, grumbling, reminiscing and attending the funerals of friends.[3]

Comfort divides ageing into two processes, physiological and sociogenic. Physiological ageing is a biological process that shows itself in physical growth and physical deterioration, although medical science can offer the means to slow down the latter. The sociogenic process is the role that our folklore, prejudices and misconceptions impose on the elderly.

Alison Norman, in her pamphlet *Aspects of Ageism*, describes the ambivalence that is at the root of people's attitudes across the generations. On the one hand, 'feelings of personal affection, a sense of duty, a desire not to hurt or reject, and a deep unconditional belief in the value of individual life, impels us to honour, protect, defend and extol the value of older people'.[4] On the other hand, there are feelings that cannot be openly expressed — such as the contempt felt for the old and weak by the young and strong, and the fear of mortality that old age represents; there is also guilt, which is translated into anger, and resentment over the need to use scarce resources or precious time on people who have 'had' their lives. Underlying these feelings is the universal truth of animal instinct, which challenges and dislodges the leader of the herd as its strength wanes. In the animal kingdom, those too weak to keep up with the young are abandoned to their fate. This animal instinct is obviously present in all of us and we ignore its effects at our peril.

However, there are some signs that stereotypes are changing, and that older people themselves are at last beginning to set the pace and agenda.

The *Independent on Sunday* (30 June 1991) reported that Research International, which serves the advertising industry, had established a 'Fifty-Something Unit' to explore the images of older people in advertising. The startling discovery had been made that the fifty-plus age group regarded themselves as virtually invisible. They buy products in spite of commercials, rather than because of them.

Traditionally, advertisers have ignored the older market. According to their reasoning, conventional wisdom states that the old are poor and set in their ways — and therefore unlikely to change brands. Supposedly, the old are not interested in being young and dynamic. And this, of course, is the only image that most companies know how to foster. Older people have all too often been depicted on commercials as doing foolish 'young' things. This has offended not only the fifty-plus age group, but all other age groups too.

Graham Staplehurst, Deputy Director of Research International, is quoted in the *Independent on Sunday* article as saying that the fifty-plus stereotypes are out of date. While it is true that the 'Depression generation' was trained in thrift, those born after 1940 grew up in the affluent 1950s and 1960s. They belong to the 'television generation' and many of them, now that their children have left home, have the freedom to enjoy wealth inherited from their parents. It is the 'Fifty-Somethings' of today who buy a large proportion of video machines and compact discs; 77 per cent own a car; and 70 per cent have a microwave. Their disposable income is estimated at £130 billion. According to Staplehurst: 'As they reach retirement, they hand back the keys to the company car and are in the market for a replacement.'

But what of those living in more straitened financial circumstances? Eric Midwinter, of the Centre for Policy on Ageing, argues that pensioners should have an income that enables them, within reason, to take part in a range of activities open to other age groups. He maintains that at present they receive a mixture of sporadic concessions and random treats. These concessions cover travel and medical care, as well as various perks in the commercial sector. Clothes can be dry-cleaned on Mondays; cheap hair-cuts are to be had on Wednesdays; the rather bleak month of November offers unlimited train journeys for a token amount. If pensioners take advantage of these special treats (and who can blame them?), they are in fact colluding with the diminished status that society imposes on them. They are letting themselves be seen (and probably seeing themselves) as a disadvantaged minority.

In the field of housing, statistics reveal that older people live in poorer housing with a lack of basic amenities. Some 7 per cent of people aged over seventy-five who live alone have no inside lavatory and, if they live in urban boroughs, there are no longer any municipal public baths.

Another myth is that elderly people are massive consumers of all the health services. In fact, the most expensive item in health-service budgets is high-technology treatment, and this is seldom available for elderly people. This age group is certainly not to blame for the present financial crisis.

The following was a letter published in the *Guardian* (3 October 1989):

> My active and young-at-heart seventy-one-year-old aunt recently sought medical treatment from the NHS for her varicose veins, which had begun to be painful. The specialist told her that she could not have the operation to replace the damaged veins with artificial ones because it was not advisable for a person of her age to have an operation. Furthermore, the operation for varicose veins was essentially a cosmetic one and therefore normally reserved for younger women who needed to keep their husbands happy. Is this official NHS policy?

Private health-insurance schemes are yet another example of the disadvantages of ageing. You join when young and healthy, hoping for protection in old age when illness may occur. But from the age of sixty onwards, the subscription starts to increase every five years. Even a scheme aimed directly at retired people pushes the cost up every four years until one reaches the age of eighty, when, it is assumed, most people have died, so it is safe to stop the increase. Most schemes obviously aim at the young and productive and are paid for by business firms because of the convenience of choosing when an executive is to be off sick. When no longer productive — that is, when one is old — much less help is available.

Older people can sometimes collude unconsciously with the young by letting themselves be treated as figures of fun, charity or patronage. In residential or hospital care, staff attitudes can lead to residents being treated as children, or even as babies. They have to submit to being ordered about, and patronized with terms such as 'Dear' or 'Ducks' or various nicknames. Respect for age seems non-existent.

One of the authors of this book was for ten years chaplain to a large hospital in East London that was originally a workhouse. The older patients remembered the hospital's origins, and resigned themselves to the circus-like atmosphere of the place. Matron's round would be immediately followed by visiting hours for families. On each occasion, the beds were lined up in straight rows, and the patients were sat up, scrubbed and clean, each with a neatly tied ribbon as a top-knot. Matron walked round, repeating her routine 'How are you?' There was no chance to reply. Matron had already moved on. Looking through the doorway into the ward, the rows of fresh-ribboned occupants resembled white-haired poodles. The relatives then arrived, whisked in, gave quick kisses and then took out bags of biscuits, fruit and sweets. Speedily, the contents were fed to the 'poodles', while each relative gossiped to the relative of the patient in the next bed.

Sadly, human nature does not change very much. Quite recently, a family visited an elderly next-of-kin in a West Country hospital. They were greeted with this request: 'If I get worse, will you please not let them give me toys.' In that same ward, at Christmas, another patient was presented by her family with a gigantic Father Christmas, which was tucked up in bed with her. The relatives no doubt felt full of seasonal good will, but the patient certainly did not.

The stereotypes are beginning to change, yet there is a hidden danger lurking in the latest image of ageing: the so-called 'recycled teenager' or 'chronologically gifted'. As an antidote to the 'passive victim', we now have denial and the refashioning of the older person as glamorous or athletic. As Anne Karpf has written (*Weekend Guardian*, 3–4 August 1991): 'Increasingly, older people are depicted not as demented crones but as leotarded achievers. Ageism hasn't gone away; it's had a face lift.' The new way of valuing older people is to highlight their youthfulness and praise them for looking young and behaving likewise. Ageing has become a social crime. Karpf stresses that the new stereotype is even more oppressive than the old one. Celebrities like Joan Collins and Jane Fonda may be admirable in their way, but they represent aspirations that are quite unattainable, or even desirable, for many older people. Also, just like the previous stereotypes, the new one still lumps people together as one category, rather than acknowledging their differences. Karpf concludes: 'It's the preoccupation with the exceptional who defy their age, and our obsession with juvenescence, that wants discarding. Peter Pan is not an appropriate icon for our greying times.'

There are moments in our lives when we seem to stand outside our bodies and are appalled at certain features — such as the age blotches on our skin — and we find ourselves frantically trying to correct them. In the same way, adolescents may resent their spottiness, yet instinctively realize that these are milestones on their journey from childhood through puberty. It is now that they may begin to grieve for the loss of childhood.

There is a common complaint that elderly people, especially those in residential care, spend much of their time comparing notes about their current aches and pains and creaky joints. This could be a misreading of what is actually happening. A shared connoisseurship of new, blemished physicality is perhaps a kind of wonder or fear. It may even be a reaffirmation of a body in which the person once took pride, but now finds less and less recognizable. There is a hard lesson to be learnt, and this has to do with 'being' body, rather than 'having' a body.

One elderly man was heard to say: 'Every morning I feel myself. If I feel warm, I get up.' There is an intense sensibility here to the fragility of life.

One seventy-year-old woman writes: 'I think the joy of old age is linked with the closeness of death. The foreshortening of the future brings a new intensity to everyday experience. I appreciate everyday things now as I rarely did in the hurly-burly of my youth — knowing they are transitory makes me value them the more.'

A hundred elderly people were asked what it was that

brought home to them the fact that they were no longer young. Here are two of the replies:

> I do not think of myself as old. There is a certain amount of dualism here, as I regard myself as my personality which inhabits a body. This body has to be looked after properly. Provided there is no gross deformity, chronic or acute illness, the personality will function well at all ages.

And:

> There is no specific date. Some are born *old*. Others are never, ever old. The latter, even when reflexes are slower and years of change or sickness or bereavement, their spirit shines through. One cannot generalize.

It seems important to listen to what old people are actually saying about themselves and it is heartening when we hear them refute the negative or unrealistic images with which society has burdened them. The refutation of those images will be one of the main themes of this book. It is up to the clergy, pastoral workers and all who care for the older generation to work against what Jung called 'the shadow' — in this case, what we deny in ourselves and attribute to others, the process known as projection. And it is just as important for the recipients of these projections to refuse to live in the shadow that we have unconsciously cast upon them. To live in this way can only lead to despair.

The 'shadow' is that part of ourselves with which we are not at ease and that we do not want to own. Without going deeply into the writings of Jung, we can surely smell danger in the denial that lies at the root of most ageist attitudes. We can also see how people at the receiving end may become both the victims and the perpetrators of the stereotypes that we have imposed on them.

The voice of Jung will crop up with a certain regularity in these pages. Not only was he intensely interested in the second half of life as a spiritual journey, but he was forever grappling with paradox. To be 'whole' was to integrate the opposites, without falling into a one-sided half-life, in which only one attitude or choice was possible. Old age is full of paradox, and another theme of this book will be to see how we can steer a course between the opposite poles of despair and celebration. Without diminishing the inevitable sorrows of old age, perhaps we shall be able to spot a few advantages — even, perhaps, a hint of that elusive quality called serenity. Who, among us — imagining that one could be given such a magical opportunity — would honestly choose to go back and relive the awkward years of youth, which would mean, of course, shedding any titbits of wisdom that we might have managed to pick up as the years have advanced?

Mercifully, perhaps, no such choice is possible and there *is* wisdom to be learnt from the old (if we would only do a bit more listening), as the following quotes will show:

> I treasure the child within me, because its curiosity, interest and outgoingness are more important to me now than ever. I value the adult I was, because her conflicts, struggles and successes have made me what I am. But I have no wish to deny being old. I am not evading the realities of death and disease. Surely the Third Age can incorporate them and become as significant as the ages that have gone before. (A seventy-year-old woman).

> We ourselves are a story with a beginning, middle and end, with moments of excitement, of fullness, of tragedy and waste, of satisfaction and of comedy. We resist the idea that this story, what we are, and how we have lived, is insignificant. We find meaning in it all through the one, who by an Incarnation, Death and Resurrection, has given us, not packaged answers, but a revelation of divine character and purpose. (An elderly priest, just before he died).

An American research anthropologist, Sharon Kaufman, has conducted a survey to find out how elderly people talk about themselves, their past, their present and their concern for the future. Here are some of her conclusions:

> I have observed that when they talk about who they are and how their lives have been, they do not speak of being old as meaningful in itself, that is they do not relate to ageing or chronological age as a category of experience or

meaning. On the contrary, when old people talk about themselves, they express a sense of self that's ageless — an identity that maintains continuity despite the physiological and social changes that come with old age.[5]

A sense of self and of continuity — these are the touchstones that old people need in order to keep a feeling of aliveness. And, for spiritual well-being, they must be able to give value to themselves so that they can give it — and also receive it — from others.

What gives human beings, whether old or young, a sense of self is the subject of Chapter 2. What makes them spiritual beings will be touched on throughout the book, and eventually we will endeavour to define this somewhat elusive spirituality that the old may be able to learn from the young, and, perhaps more often, can be shown to the young by the old — but only if the young do not turn away.

We must not be blinkered. The old are not ugly — it is simply that we have been taught that only youth has beauty. If beauty is in the eye of the beholder, perhaps we need to wipe our eyes and change our focus.

The following poem by Ernest Rhys describes how old people see themselves:

> We old men,
> We are not what we seem
> As we go down the street.
>
> In our old eyes
> Shine boyhood memories:
> We have seen horses swerve,
> And vessels sail,
> We know the crimson curve
> Upon a young girl's cheek.
>
> When we wake at end of night,
> We draw a deeper breath
> And hail the Lord of Light.
> We are not what we seem,
> We are not afraid of death
> As we go down the street.[6]

Notes

1. S. Green, *Nursing Times*, 14–20 August 1991.
2. ibid.
3. A. Comfort, *A Good Age*, Michael Beazley 1977, p. 24.
4. A. Norman, *Aspects of Ageism*, Centre for Policy on Ageing 1987, p. 3.
5. S. R. Kaufman, *The Ageless Self*, Meridian 1986, p. 7.
6. E. Rhys, 'The Old Men', in *Poems of Our Time, 1900–1941*, Dent 1945.

TWO

Loss and Gain —
The Changing Experience of 'Self'

<hr>

If I am not for myself, who will be? And if I am
only for myself, what am I?
Hillel

But now I only know I am — that's all.
John Clare

When writing about 'Self', especially with a capital letter, we
need to remember that the concept is impossible to define; it
gets used, both in writing and speech, in all sorts of different
ways. This chapter will attempt to explore some of these
ambiguities. All we can really be sure about is self-experience:
that which distinguishes us as being conscious and consciously
human. The sense of 'being' or 'having' a self, in a world of
other selves, fluctuates throughout life and is susceptible to
all sorts of influences. Although we mostly take ourselves for
granted, there are sure to be moments of crisis when the
experience is all but lost. Ageing, as a time of change, can all
too easily shake our confidence in who we are.

Viewed from the outside, the old have everything to lose
and nothing to gain. Today's culture is centred on youth, and
old people are only praised if they manage to look young for
their age. The effort to sustain a false identity becomes a
losing battle. When youth only is valued, age becomes
pathological: a terminal disease. A person *seen* to be useless
all too easily conforms to this image, and thus *becomes*
useless. Self-esteem (or perhaps more accurately 'ego esteem')
can scarcely be maintained in the face of another generation's
non-recognition. We cannot become mature human beings all

15

on our own. Our sense of what we are has as much to do with what we are for others as for ourselves alone. For most of us, the first 'other' is the mother. As infants, we need to be mirrored in her eyes, so that she gives us recognition and we can slowly grow and become individual, while keeping the gift of her continuing presence inside us. Without this 'internalized' mother, there will be no reflection of what we are, and we are left, like Narcissus, with nothing but an empty pool that mirrors our own nothingness.

Learning to relate is hard and a child spends a long time as a totally dependent being, only slowly separating what belongs to his or her own inside from differentiated others in an outer world — an outer world that will not always fit in with his or her wishes. Growing up takes a long time. It feels slow. The years stretch towards unimaginably distant horizons. Later, as we mature, time (or our perception of it) accelerates. We get caught up in achievements, rearing families, and all sorts of business and busyness. Adults, especially young adults, are made to feel important. They contribute to society and society values them. It is easy to feel cut off from our fumbling beginnings, although our children, if we can identify with them, may remind us. Or neurosis may sometimes (even usefully) unite us with our past. Or we may have to wait for the slowing down that comes with age to feel childlike again and experience that sense of continuity so essential to selfhood.

The old and the very young may ask themselves the same sort of questions: 'Who am I?' 'Why am I in the world?' They may even attempt to answer each other's questions. But whereas the child will most likely be curious about where he came from, the old person may begin to wonder where he is going. His horizons, though still unimaginable, are no longer distant.

How, at any age, can any of us answer the question 'Who am I?' The self that we can touch, feel and partly see is the body. We are aware of an inside and an outside and of our skin, both as a protective covering and as a sensitive receiver of external influences. We are not aware of all that goes on internally and our own hidden organs will always be something of a mystery. Even if we study physiology or become surgeons, the bodies under investigation will belong to other people. The workings of our own remain unseen. Because bodies occupy a bounded space but move about in a wider world, we get an idea of our human limitations. Infants, gently held and protected, are most probably under the illusion that there are no limitations, but they soon have to let go of such omnipotence.

Throughout our lives, we tend to regard our bodies as private property in which we locate not only the unseen organs that give us good or bad feelings depending on how well they work, but also, so it seems, our thoughts and dreams. There may be cultural variations as to whether we place our minds in our heads or our feelings in our hearts, but some sort of inside location probably makes us feel comfortably integrated as human beings.

A group of children who were asked to make drawings of their souls (without defining what the word meant to them) placed their souls in all sorts of positions both inside and outside the body; they drew them in various shapes and colours and of differing sizes. Some saw them as a white lining under the skin taking up the whole body space. Others showed a separate entity which came and went in much the same way as some ethnic groups believe they have many souls, or that their souls leave their bodies when they dream.

The earliest dreams recalled by one individual were of her bodily products — the interesting but forbidden pickings from her nose which had been called 'bogeys'. In the dreams, these 'bogey men' took on a life of their own and lived in underground passages where she would wander and get lost or feel they were after her. The inside and outside of herself must have been confused or not securely established.

Interest in our bodies and what goes in and out of them persists into old age; the reassurance of the familiar alternates with changes that may be too frightening to accept unless the sense of self, and especially continuity of being, has been well formed and strengthened early in life.

How, then, does this sense of being a self develop?

Its elusive nature is complicated by the fact that, in any

study of self, the investigator is, at the same time, the subject and the object of his examination. We are not observing creatures on another planet, nor even our nextdoor neighbours, but our own thoughts, feelings and sensations. If we do not rely on what our own experience teaches, we will get lost in a maze of theories.

We have seen that, even in childhood, each individual varies in how far to separate soul and body. Much Christian teaching tends to encourage a split — especially when the 'bad' body is contrasted with the 'good' soul, and Jesus Christ is not allowed to be incarnate. The doctrine of 'The Resurrection of the Body' should be seen as an attempt to heal this split; but crude pictures of the Last Judgement, with corpses leaping from graves, discourage most of us from taking this idea seriously, even as an allegory of wholeness restored.

In talking about soul and body, we need to be careful about terminology. Theologically, we are accustomed to the word 'soul' being the immaterial or immortal part of man. Thus soul transcends body in something like the same way as, in Jung's psychology, the self transcends the ego. In everyday speech, we usually limit what we mean by the word 'self' to our individual consciousness, with only a dim realization that there is more to our experience than we actually know at any given moment. In fact, we are used to living with a very fragmented picture of who we are. St Paul states: 'Now I know in part . . .', but always with the hope of some future understanding (which implies more than what is usually meant by *conscious* understanding), 'then shall I know even also as I am known' (1 Corinthians 13.12).

Turning again to Jung, we need, in youth, to build a strong ego, meaning that individual sense of 'I am' which enables us to live independently without too many props and to know that we are doing so. The ego, according to Jung, is the centre of consciousness, but it is only one aspect of the self's totality. In human development, the self is the home from which we start, but it is also our ultimate goal. Here are some words from an early follower of Jung: 'It is as though, in attaining ego-consciousness, we become born psychologically, we come forth from the womb of the unconscious, but in the discovery of the self we become twice-born and enter a larger world; we are born again'.[1] There are echoes here of Christ's reply to Nicodemus, when the latter asked how a man can be born when he is old: 'That which is born of the flesh is flesh; and that which is born of the Spirit is spirit' (John 3.6).

Jung set us the task of individuation — that is, the realization of our full potential, the finding of our 'selves' — and he saw it as especially important in the second half of life. 'The ego', he wrote, 'stands to the self as the moved to the mover.'[2] This mover, which we may want to call God, has no definition because it transcends our conceptual frames and eludes all efforts at capture.

So we find ourselves using the language of images, the language of Jung's archetypes, those inherited predispositions that are unknowable in themselves but which trigger off in all of us such powerful imagery that our lives are touched at moments of crisis and transition with paradoxes of good/bad, dark/light, love/hate, and these are often personified as awesome, terrifying or comforting figures. Thus we have the self-image and its shadow-opposite, and the God-image, which also has its dark side, usually depicted as the devil. If we avoid unacceptable parts of our being, we may find ourselves leading blinkered lives; this means that much of our potential creativity goes to waste. Those Christians who rob Christ of his shadow divest him of his humanity. It is interesting that when Dostoevsky, in his novel entitled *The Idiot*, set out to invent a Christ-like man, he came up with an indecisive weakling who needed a shadow figure, like a twin, whom he both loved and hated but could not be parted from. The Gospels do not describe a gentle Jesus, but a puzzling, contradictory character who speaks to us in riddles and often brings, not peace, but the sword.

In facing the paradoxes of our ageing, we need to be wary of one-sided attitudes. For some, it is all gloom and a useless looking back to the pleasures of youth. Others simply deny their diminishing powers and strive to compete with their juniors. In facing reality, the opposites will always hang in a fine balance and neither side should be overlooked.

There are many archetypal images of old people. These
range from wise men with silver beards and twinkling eyes to
dribbling, dirty tramps; from comfortable grannies to
toothless witches. These are not rounded human beings but
display limited aspects of our humanity. Redfearn, in his
book entitled *My Self, My Many Selves*, referred to such
personifications as sub-personalities, like actors who move in
and out of the spotlight: 'The feeling of "I" . . . may inhabit
one role for a moment, then another . . . some people are
stuck in one role much of the time . . .'[3] He then asks, since
we are all many, how can we be one? In our search for
wholeness, there must be a considerable letting go of roles
that we find ourselves outgrowing. The self-centredness
(narcissism) of infancy has to decrease in order that love of
others can grow. Conversely, later in life we may need to let
go of clinging to the people we love so that something new
can enter our lives. If we are to live creatively, it is no use
following the same patterns that were appropriate at a
younger age. If the old live simply for the young (comforting
as it may feel to be needed), they will most likely find
themselves exploited and then begin to resent it. Nostalgia
gets more painful with age and can turn to bitterness.

It is undoubtedly easier to accept the loss of what we have
loved and enjoyed than the fantasy of what never became
real. Those who most resent their ageing are often those who
feel that they have been overlooked. One woman said of her
maiden aunt, 'Her illness is that nothing ever happened to
her.' These deprived people can often destroy the help that
others try to give them because of their own extreme envy.
What they, themselves, have never received, they can now
neither accept nor give.

The old, like the very young, may feel that life, or God, is
'jolly unfair'. In outward terms, they may well be right, but,
however hard the knocks of fate, it seems important to realize
that, inwardly, there is always a modicum of choice. Even in
the face of severe depression, phrases like 'I'm made that
way' or 'It's all in the genes' turn people into fossils. Such
attitudes need to be questioned, doubted and turned upside
down if the sufferers are to be freed. Awareness of even

infinitessimal choice opens the way to a true 'self-conscious-ness', a consciousness that the pain, depression or deprivation is a part and not the whole of who that person truly is.

We do not have to accept diminishment by stoical self (or ego)-denial, but merely to let go, gently and at the appropriate time, of earlier attitudes and attachments — rather in the way that we send to jumble sales the clothes that no longer fit. Old age is not all diminishment. Wisdom, even if unacknowledged by the young, accompanies our failing faculties and probably few would willingly exchange this hard-earned wisdom for the ignorance of youth.

Many of the older generation, if not too hampered by disabilities, have a chance to enjoy a new freedom. After all, there is nobody senior to lay down the law. The choices are at last one's own. Although there may be a struggle as to whether freedom or loneliness wins, this can be a time for all sorts of explorations, either in the outer or inner world (or both), a time perhaps to compensate for what was missed earlier, a time even for a little self-interest, what we might call a 'healthy narcissism'. When Jung wrote, 'every man who pursues his own goals is a narcissist',[4] he was not using the term in a pathological sense. Without a strong ego, built on the love given to us by others, we cannot afford compassion for our fellow humans, nor can we easily let go of any part of what we think of as ourselves. And, in the end, of course, there has to be a lot of letting go.

Teilhard de Chardin put it this way: '. . . you must first of all *be* . . . you must develop yourself and take possession of the world in *order to be*. Once this has been accomplished, then is the time to think about renunciation; then is the time to accept diminishment for the sake *of being in another*.'[5] This last phrase, 'being in another', is somewhat mysterious. To live 'in God', or 'not I, but Christ liveth in me' (Galatians 2.20), would look to some of us like losing our identities. The question arises, what part of our identity do we lose, the 'ego' or the 'self'? Teilhard has urged us, in youth, to *be*. He does not make Jung's distinction between 'ego' and 'self', but, in his own words, seems to refer to a widening of experience, only attainable after some painful letting go of what we have achieved in the prime of life. This may be seen as Jung's goal of sacrificing the ego in service of the self.

The mystics, in all ages, seem able both to let go of their egos and also to get straight through to the reality behind the images, as, for instance, the fourteenth-century author of *The Cloud of Unknowing* and Meister Eckhart, who declared, in such a straightforward way, that 'God is neither this nor that'.6 He applied the same statement to ourselves. We are neither this nor that. We are not what we think we are. His equivalent of Jung's individuation is the birth of God in the soul, a birth that does not deny the world and the flesh. Those who experience it are 'turned toward this birth with everything they possess be it never so earthy'.7 They can then see creation through God's eyes and are themselves transparent to God, or rather 'a Ground of Godhead', 'God beyond God'.8 It is interesting how often, at crucial stages in our lives, we tend to dream of birth, often of a special or 'divine' child. Jung saw the child archetype as a mediator between conscious and unconscious and as a symbol of wholeness.

Yet it is this wholeness, supposedly our ultimate goal, that older people are most afraid of losing. When bodies start disintegrating and abilities diminish, they do not feel particularly whole. And, although it is no doubt true that continuing exercise of both mind and muscle ('if you don't want to lose it, use it'), together with positive thinking, may keep us going longer than resigning ourselves to fate, there must come a time when the fight becomes unrealistic. Anxiety, denial, and trying to hide failure and handicap can only lead to depression.

The old look to the young for reassurance, not for lies. Weakness of sight, hearing and memory — all these need to be faced and accepted. Some failings can of course be overcome. Hearing aids are getting smaller, lighter, and easier to use. Cataract operations can be performed on nonagenarians. Sometimes the recovery of sight seems little short of a miracle and the old see colours with the eyes of childhood, remembering a long-forgotten brilliance. For one old person, a pot of marmalade became a crock of gold.

It is well known that memory for recent events becomes

vague, whereas memories of long ago remain as vivid as ever. Sometimes dates get confused. One old lady kept saying to her daughter, 'You remember, Darling, before the war . . .' The daughter had to answer with a question, 'Which war?' It was nearly always the first, 1914–18. Luckily both mother and daughter were able to laugh at the muddle.

Sometimes those who become forgetful are afraid of senility. They want reassurance, yet get tired of being fobbed off with half-truths and evasive answers. A dialogue with an elderly patient in therapy went something like this:

PATIENT: Truthfully — you must have noticed my loss of memory.

THERAPIST: Yes.

PATIENT: Why didn't you say so?

THERAPIST: Because you never asked.

PATIENT: People keep telling me not to worry — that they forget things too. But it's no good pretending. I'm getting worse.

THERAPIST: Yes.

PATIENT: Well, at least you admit it.

THERAPIST: What seems worst for you is your anxiety about forgetting — like a feeling of shame. I've got a feeling you still remember what's important to you.

PATIENT: Oh — don't just be like all the others — trying to make me feel better. What d'you mean — important?

THERAPIST: I mean perhaps you were never much good at remembering practical things.

PATIENT: So I'm a scatterbrain. [Here they both laughed.]

THERAPIST: Did they call you that as a child?

PATIENT: Yes, all the time.

THERAPIST: And did that worry you?

PATIENT: Oh no. I had better things to think about.

THERAPIST: Perhaps that's still true. But you feel you can't be the rebellious child any more, standing up to parents, thinking you know better. I think you're afraid of being thought a poor old lady.

She acknowledged this fear, together with relief that at least one person did not regard her as on the way to dementia. This conversation echoes Dr Johnson's words to Boswell: 'There is a wicked inclination in most people to suppose an old man decayed in his intellects. If a young man or middleaged man, when leaving a company, does not recollect where he left his hat, it is nothing; but if the same inattention is discovered in an old man, people will shrug up their shoulders and say, "His memory is going." '9

How others see us, and how we *see* others seeing us, must influence the way we see ourselves and this is where a sense of continuity is of such importance — even if this means that our own awareness of what we are is at variance with other people's. These others see us only now in our ageing bodies and witness our ageing behaviour. Our own sense of ourselves includes both past and present — not in separate bits, but as a unity. In so far as experience is fragmented, the fragments come and go. Wholeness can never be present in consciousness all at once and at the same time, nor can we remain conscious for ever. Our memories are part of our identity. But, although we need to remember, we also need to forget. Without forgetting, we 'would be suffocated in an infinite ocean of images'.10 Forgetting is part of the letting go, so necessary if we are to move on to new experience. In letting go of our limited egos, we do not let go of ourselves, those selves that transcend the polarities of conscious/unconscious, remembering/forgetting; or, following Jung, that 'Self' that 'occupies the central position of authority in relation to psychological life and, therefore, the destiny of the individual'.11

As we move towards our final letting go, we may feel not quite at home in our bodies. This in itself is not peculiar to age. The young anorexic has a distorted idea of what her body looks like and she works hard to get it under control. In extreme cases, men think they are women in the wrong bodies (and vice versa) and resort to surgery to bring about a change. Bereavement can feel like amputation, as though the metaphor of one flesh is factual. In losing a marriage partner, we also lose the person who is still in touch with our youth and sexuality. As old friends die, we have to rely only on our own experience of all that we have been and still are.

Letting go of some of our activities, for instance on retirement, means having time for reflection. Perhaps there is 'homework' to be done: reconciliation, forgiveness and realizing our need to be forgiven. It may be too late for any active reparation, but perhaps we can resolve our problems in our own minds or at least accept what cannot be resolved. This is a job to do before we become too tired or incapable. It is a time for tidying our material possessions and giving some of them away, for putting our inner world in order and generally getting rid of clutter.

Mind and body tend to age at different rates and this may seem to separate them. To the young in mind, the body becomes a faulty apparatus, not always responsive to the will. To some this might be the first intimation of having (or being) a soul, a more enduring 'me' than the worn-out machinery we have to inhabit. Yet for the only kind of life we know, our bodies, however ill-functioning, are necessary. We may rage at them, abuse them, pity them and long to restore them to youth and vitality, yet we also, most of the time, feel some sort of love for our bodies because they are so exclusively our own. Chronic pain as an everyday experience, though not exactly welcome, becomes part of what we recognize, a reminder that we are alive. A man in his seventies wrote an ode to his pain. It was not great poetry, but a way of cursing an enemy with whom he gradually became acquainted and eventually could treat as a friend. But, beyond a certain point, pain or illness can become so consuming that all we have left to know of ourselves is the bit that hurts or feels sick. The hope is that, in moments of remission, there can still be some awareness, however dim, of a wholeness that embraces more than the flagging ego. St Paul wrote that though 'our outward man perish, yet the inward man is renewed day by day' (2 Corinthians 4.16).

If the brain (which, unlike the mind, is part of the body) gets damaged or decays before the heart and lungs stop working, communication comes to a halt and the 'self' that has been loved and cared for is hard to identify. We continue to look after the body without knowing where the 'person' is.

Looking at figures in the day room of an average old people's home, we may be aware both of passivity and bustle. It is the attendants who bustle. Their youthful way of being is to be active. They are disconcerted by any lack of alertness to what goes on in the world, even that limited institutional world with its attempts at homely prettiness. It needs a mature sensitivity to imagine a rich inner experience that is never going to be shared. All too often the best intentioned carers treat the old like children, either 'good' or 'naughty' according to their participation in the rather artificial happenings built into their daily routine. There may, by now, be little choice left for the wheel-chaired, hard-of-hearing, partially sighted inhabitants, but any quiet decision not to join in should be respected. Who knows what secret process of individuation or birth of God in the soul may be pursuing its hidden course? Do these drooping figures suffer in their silence? Suffering may be part of their task, but they do not necessarily suffer less when we try to force on them a younger person's standards of normality. Even if written off as demented, why not let them dement, dream or meditate in peace? Forceful arousal may, for all we know, feel like being dragged back from a near-death experience. They may even be choosing to let go and die in their own way and in their own time.

The unconscious is said to be timeless, spaceless and does not obey the laws of logic or grammar, but it is still life. In reality we spend more time unconscious than conscious. It is curious that many people who believe in a life after the body's death have so little respect for life in a demented body. In fact, we know as little about the former as the latter. What we can be pretty sure about is that most of our recognizable identity — what each of us claims as 'I' — has eventually to be surrendered:

> One modest mortal
> In the teeming swarm of life.
> One lifetime stretch

In creation's endless span
On one finite sphere
Of a vast infinity.
How can it be
Of importance that
I am?[12]

We know the Christian answer: that each individual is unique in God's sight. It is a comfort to many, but for others belief alternates with doubt. Watching people die often reminds us of the struggle before birth. Socrates, as well as Jesus, was convinced that death was not final. Jung, questioned in his eighties as to whether he believed in life after death, refused to 'believe' anything without evidence, but trusted in the unconscious of old people which seems to see no limits beyond space and time. Without denying death, those approaching it seem able to treat it not as an end but as a beginning. To behave as though we will continue through the centuries seemed to Jung the proper way to live.[13] Theologians and others grapple with this question. If the answer were easy to understand, would it be worth knowing? Whatever happens to the self must surely be the ultimate surprise.

Jung's ideas have appealed to many Christians, but others see him as turning orthodoxy upside down. If the old are childlike enough to wonder and be ready for change, they may be excited by the questions he poses. Some prefer to revert to the prayers learnt at Mother's knee. Both attitudes need to be respected. There is often a tendency in old age to go back to the spiritual tradition of one's upbringing, although some people try to fight against such regression. A Jewish lady in her eighties, who had not seen the inside of a synagogue in years, remarked to a friend that she hoped she would not weaken on her deathbed and recite the Shema ('Hear O Israel the Lord thy God is One . . .'). Her friend hoped she would, as a way of letting go of her rebellion and reconnecting her with her roots.

Hospital chaplains and parish priests encounter all sorts of people — the lapsed, the unbaptized, and those who have never felt any need for religion. There are also quite a few nominal Christians who wish that, in times of trouble, the 'vicar' would include them in his calls. Ministry to the unbelieving could be seen as a challenge, but not necessarily a challenge to convert. Atheists and agnostics surely deserve pastoral care as much as regular communicants or observant Jews. Sometimes the priest, whether he likes it or not, may be the one most available to take on this responsibility.

One life-long agnostic had a stroke which deprived him of movement and speech, turning him into a captive audience. In this case, the parish priest did take up the challenge and read formal prayers at the bedside. A friend read poetry. Another, who knew him less intimately, sat with him in silence. There is no way of telling for certain which ministry was most appropriate to the dying man's needs, but perhaps the person who kept silent paid most respect to his mysteriously unique 'I-am-ness'.

Notes

1. F. G. Wickes, *The Inner World of Man*, Henry Holt, New York 1938, p. 116.
2. C. G. Jung, *The Collected Works*, 11, eds H. Read, M. Fordham, G. Adler and W. McGuire, tr. R. Hull, Routledge & Kegan Paul, p. 391.
3. J. W. T. Redfearn, *My Self, My Many Selves*, Academic Press 1985, p. 117.
4. Jung, *Collected Works*, 15, p. 102.
5. P. Teilhard de Chardin, *Le Milieu Divin*, Collins 1960, p. 78.
6. C. Smith, *The Way of Paradox: Spiritual Life as Taught by Meister Eckhart*, Darton, Longman & Todd 1987, p. 45.
7. ibid., p. 100.
8. ibid.
9. J. Boswell, *The Life of Doctor Johnson*, Methuen 1991.
10. G. Adler, *Dynamics of Self*, Coventure 1979, p. 120.
11. A. Samuels, B. Shorter, A. Plaut, *A Critical Dictionary of Jungian Analysis*, Routledge 1986, p. 135.
12. G. Scott, 'Counter Ego', in *Later Poems*, Envoi Publications, Newport.
13. C. G. Jung, 'Face to Face' with John Freeman, BBC 1958.

THREE

Sex and after Sex — Something New

An agéd man is but a paltry thing,
A tattered coat upon a stick unless
Soul clap its hands and sing . . .
W. B. Yeats

In a recent survey, 100 people in the over-sixty-five age group were asked to comment on the advantages and disadvantages of getting old. Only one admitted to missing sex and added, 'Dare I mention it?' How does this reflect the attitude of our society and the expectations, or rather non-expectations, the young have of the old?

A few generations ago, few people discussed sex except in secret, or strictly between men, but there was no taboo on talking about dying. Deathbeds and funerals featured dramatically in Victorian everyday life. In the twentieth century, however, death became unmentionable; but now, as we move towards the twenty-first century, the taboos are changing yet again. There is suddenly quite an obsession with death, and it is discussed far more freely. In contrast, although we have lived through the permissive society and every aspect of sex has been freely discussed, there is still one aspect of this subject that is largely taboo. Dare we mention it?

If the old are sexually active or have erotic fantasies, the young would rather not know. For the small child, sex is a secret. In old age, life seems to come full circle. Once more the door is closed. A ninety-year-old asked her daughter a simple question, 'What is this new disease called AIDS?' The answer was almost as evasive as the one she had herself given to this

daughter many years before when asked for some facts about
procreation. Children are nowadays given 'sex education' and
learn a lot about human biology quite early in their lives. It
takes time to link fact with feeling, and they are probably still
uneasy about what actually goes on in the parental bedroom
— but at least some of it can be openly talked about. It is now
the old (yesterday's unenlightened children) who are treated
as though they have forgotten or have never known the
secret. Signs of sexual liveliness are acceptable as long as
they can be turned into jokes. To acknowledge any strong
desire seems somehow to be against the rules. It is doubtful if
old people can even share their feelings with each other,
unless they are fortunate enough to have marriage partners
with some libido left. Sex is permissible within marriage, but
is generally assumed to disappear soon after OAP status is
reached. All too easily, the old can go along with this
assumption. This is especially true of women. Old men
sometimes pride themselves on their sexual prowess, even
though society may regard them as 'dirty old men'. Perhaps
this pride covers a dread of impotence.

Developmental changes such as the menopause do not
happen overnight, nor are they purely of the body. Being
human, we are psychosomatic creatures, with our minds and
bodies inextricably intertwined. Intercourse between humans
does not only have the procreation of children as its purpose
and couples often continue to make love in later life regardless
of their lack of fertility. Masturbation is likely to be a lonely
and second-best activity but may nevertheless bring comfort
and some sense of fulfilment — with its rich fantasy
transcending mere bodily release of tension.

Old longings persist and need expression. If unacknowledged, the body may monopolize the soul and produce
symptoms — hence a so-called 'eroticization' of vegetative
functions, appetite, digestion and sleep, so that these become
the only gratifications; or, more uncomfortably, there may be
a preoccupation with illness, which sometimes becomes the
chief topic of conversation, with old people competing with
one another in their physical ailments.

Yeats, in the lines quoted at the beginning of the chapter,

told us to clap our hands and sing, not with our bodies but with our souls. He likened the old, if they had no souls, to scarecrows with nothing inside them.[1] Singing with the soul might be seen as a forward movement, not necessarily away from the body but perhaps towards a more total way of living that gives meaning to all that we have been and are to become. We cannot experience soul without body. Whatever else we are, we can only know ourselves as embodied. When a woman of sixty-five told her therapist, somewhat wistfully, that she wanted to 'sing in her vagina', she was painfully aware of what could no longer be fulfilled. Her husband, meanwhile, was quietly mourning his own loss of potency. Both felt isolated, too proud and also too shy to communicate their feelings to each other and thereby make possible a new kind of intimacy less linked with giving each other orgasms. It was time to move on, but useless to try and force the pace. It is unlikely that any marriage will be harmonious enough for both partners to keep perfectly in step through all the bumpy transitions of their ageing.

What is lost in this painful movement to another stage of life is of course invisible and likely to go unnoticed. There may be little that any helper can do or say, but denial of old people's sexuality is bound to affect attitudes towards them. No one wants to be 'written off' as a separate species, devoid of passion. It should be obvious that for widows and widowers loss of sex, even if intercourse has given way to a less specific physical closeness, leaves an enormous gap. There will never again be quite the intimacy that takes time to mature through years of togetherness, during which the early excitement has never been entirely lost but adds poignancy to later acceptance of each other's ageing. Anticipating inevitabe change, the nineteenth-century poet Thomas Moore was able to write: 'And round the dear ruin each wish of my heart would entwine itself verdantly still.' In these lines, the young lover romantically looked ahead and vowed undying fidelity. Those getting older need both to look back and ahead so as to accept that 'ruin' of the body is not the whole story and may well accompany new growth in the soul.

One of the few novelists who has dared to describe old

lovers actually making love is Gabriel Garcia Márquez. *Love in the Time of Cholera* is about the uncertainties, but also the satisfactions, of two elderly people who had loved each other chastely in their youth and had then been parted through choice and circumstance, only to come together sexually in their seventies. At first the situation was unsatisfactory. He saw her wrinkled body, but he still loved her as the beautiful girl she had once been. He got over-excited and unable to perform: '"It's dead", he said.' Then he went to his own bed. Later, 'His beginner's haste made her shiver with compassion.' Marquez describes him as though he were still the adolescent boy whose courtship had been long ago rejected. As for the heroine:

> It was the first time she had made love in over twenty years and she had been held back by the curiosity concerning how it would feel at her age after so long a respite. But he had not given her time to find out if her body loved him too. It had been hurried and sad. . . . They did not try to make love again until much later, when the inspiration came to them without looking for it. They were satisfied with the simple joy of being together.[2]

Here there is no looking ahead. The lovers are locked in a fantasy of 'for ever'. As the boat carries them back and forth along the same stretch of river, the lovers can only repeat themselves and there is no end to their story.

This passage shows that, however much older people long for physical intimacy, full intercourse may no longer occur easily. A widow in her eighties was approached by an old flame who wanted to share her bed. She told him gently that whatever they had experienced in youth could no longer be resurrected. Afterwards she confided in a friend, 'I can't get up to that sort of thing, not with my arthritis.' It was clear that she used to enjoy 'that sort of thing' and felt nostalgic about past delights, but was able to accept her body's limitations. She was lonely sometimes, and missed cooking for a household of people. She also missed driving and going for long country walks. She would sit still more than formerly, just thinking about her life and trying to make sense of its

pattern. But she would also get restless as though looking for
something. She envied a friend who got comfort from
churchgoing, but did not think religion was what she wanted.
Jung, mysteriously, declared that a person trying to live
exclusively through the body must be unconsciously in the
grip of the spirit.[3] It is questionable whether this old lady
would have admitted to being in the grip of anything labelled
as 'spirit', but undoubtedly, as her body weakened, she was
trying to move beyond its desires.

In this case, there were children and grandchildren and
memories of an enjoyable sexuality. But not all old ladies are
so fortunate. For some, there is no fulfilled life to move
beyond. How can one leave behind what one never had? A
spinster in a geriatric ward confided in her occupational
therapist that she often did 'naughty things'. Being single and
belonging to a non-permissive generation, she was almost
certainly a virgin and had spent her life doing 'naughty
things' alone. It is sad that she should have felt so much
shame. Having no one to touch, she had needed to touch
herself and this had probably brought her a little comfort and
sense of well-being. It would be easy to label her as fixated at
an auto-erotic stage, but that would be condemnatory. No one
stage of development is neatly replaced by another and there
is probably some regression to infantile behaviour in all
sexual activity. This lonely ninety-year-old was cut off from
any affectionate caressing. Bedridden, in a ward with only
the senile for company, and her own memories getting
confused, she knew at least that her arthritic fingers were
engaged in making a woolly ball for a baby not yet born. She
would ask questions and was full of wonder about that baby
and the young couple soon to give birth. When the ball was
made, she threw it joyfully in the air, played with it and
fondled its softness. She was delighted with her small creation
and that it was a gift for one who was due to live when she
was gone.

For quite a few people, there can be no fulfilment except
that which fantasy can give. There was no meeting of bodies
in the story of that ageing voyeur, Aschenbach, in Thomas
Mann's *Death in Venice*. Imagination held him back.

Imagination also transformed the sordid into the poetic. There was certainly a yearning to touch the beautiful Tadzio, but Aschenbach did not risk such intrusion and there is only a hint that the boy knew his secret:

> The sight of this living figure, virginally pure and austere, with dripping locks, beautiful as a tender young god, emerging from the depth of the sea and sky, outrunning the element — it conjured up mythologies, it was like a primeval legend handed down from the beginning of time, of the birth of form, of the origin of the gods. With closed lids Aschenbach listened to this poesy hymning itself silently within him, and anon he thought it was good to be here and that he would stop awhile.[4]

The passion is certainly of the body, but also a source of creativity. 'The sun', he wrote, 'beguiles our attention from things of the intellect to fix it on things of the sense . . . the soul for very pleasure forgets its actual state, to cling with doting on the loveliest of all the objects she shines on . . . it is only through the medium of some corporeal being that it can raise itself again to contemplation of higher things.'[5] The lover and the artist are thus united in this 'regressive' homosexual fantasy. Nostalgia is perhaps a more apt word than regression. There must have been a longing not so much to *have* as to *be* the beautiful boy, symbol of the artist's lost youth.

A retired social worker got caught up in the same obsession and found himself following an unknown teenager through the streets. Watching was enough. Any notion of acting out his fantasies seemed to him not only irresponsible, but absurd. The boy's existence added new excitement to his life and he was thankful, before he died, to have known at last the heady experience of being in love. Such episodes are reminiscent of adolescent hero-worship and have an unexpected purity. So little is asked of the beloved, merely his (or her) continued, though distant, presence, making it 'good to be here and . . . stop awhile'.

Although claiming to be liberated, our society often seems peculiarly blinkered, conforming not to the propriety of our ancestors, but to a notion that sex is for the young and beautiful, the ones who are able to use it as a means of increasing the population — even though many are trying hard *not* to do so. The norm is still heterosexual, young and family-oriented. Some deviation may be tolerated in youth, but increasingly deplored (even if unconsciously) in those judged to be past their prime.

The question remains unanswered and perhaps unanswerable: what can old people do with their sexuality?

It seems that eventually biology is kind. The urgency of sexual desire and its gratification becomes more diffuse and, as our bodies start letting us down, we have, whether we like it or not, to get used to living with our longings unsatisfied. One might even see hunger as a healthier state than satiation. The more we desire, the more we reach beyond ourselves, and, when sex ceases to satisfy, we find other means of solace. The 'oceanic' experience of bliss may come to be discovered in less specific ways than sexual orgasm. Listening to music, sitting in the sun and smelling the flowers, looking at the stars, the elusive movement between sleep and waking — all these may bring moments of union, as though with something beyond our familiar consciousness.

But no state of bliss lasts long and, just as loneliness often follows sexual intercourse, there continues to be a swing between the opposites of fusion and separation. The old seldom achieve an uninterrupted serenity. In fact, they have been described as 'constantly struggling between childhood recollections and confrontation with the end of existence';[6] also, as having dialogues between their earlier and later identities. Sexually, we can be infantile at any age, wanting to be held and cuddled. As older children, making new discoveries, we are more interested in separating than cuddling, and our energy, not yet defined by us as sexual, flows freely in all sorts of directions. Before puberty polarizes us into extremes of male and female, we may feel almost genderless — just people. If this freedom comes back to us in old age, it will be enhanced, as well as confused, by a kaleidoscope of memories whose many facets give colour to our moods.

A curious melange of 'childhood recollections' and the 'end of existence' was reflected in a dream reported by a woman in her sixties who was mourning both husband and mother. She dreamed that a professor made a pattern on the floor with pieces of junk. The pattern took on a female shape and he called it 'The Mother'. A child ran about, laughing and playing and sometimes screaming. Then the pieces were rearranged and the body's organs displaced. The child changed from a boy into a girl. The dreamer was watching the scene, yet also partly identified with the child. She woke in a state of confusion and it was not easy to see clearly the many facets that her dream, so surprisingly, threw together. There seems to have been a childish curiosity, tinged with fear, about what was going on in the mother's body and also the role of this mysteriously powerful professor. There was certainly a hint of panic about death and the body's dissolution into pieces of junk. As for her own identity, was she male, female, young or old?

Old people's dreams often resemble children's in being overwhelming. They are also peopled with dead friends and lovers who tend to be ill or unable to speak. Sometimes the dreamer tries to bring the dead to life, and this may mean holding a limp penis or simply sharing body warmth. Often a secret is about to be revealed, but is lost on waking. But some of these dreams are touched with joy. A widow dreamed that she was able to spend a weekend with her husband in Rome, knowing that he was dead and they only had these few days together. The dream was bathed in golden, sunset light. She called it 'The Eternal City' and knew that was where her husband belonged, but that she must return to a darker world. Some old women dream of having babies, a nostalgic return to the past, or a longing for what they never had, but also a hope for the future, for the advent of something new, a rebirth.

Images of birth may save us from the fruitless search for more and more of the same gratification. Pleasure as a habit will soon get less pleasurable and the seeker gets caught in a closed circle as if chasing his own tail. Substitutes for sex — drink, food, drugs — are not the answer. Sublimation is a way of desexualizing or diverting the procreative energy into more appropriate channels. Transformation is another term that carries a hint of something more creative. One thinks of the butterfly freeing itself from the worn-out chrysalis, a symbol of resurrection.

In each individual there are potentialities for being both male and female but, in early adulthood, the sexes tend to be poles apart, yet complementing and compensating each other, particularly at the time of giving birth and nurturing the next generation. During pregnancy and when the baby is helpless, the mother is gentle and protective and curbs her aggressive tendencies, which she may even express vicariously through her husband. He, in turn, needs to give up passive dependence on a mother figure and show himself strong, active, reliable. When two people live together for a long time, patterns develop between them and become fixed, with each partner colluding with the other to keep up a way of life that may persist longer than is necessary. Each will take on different responsibilities and jobs are divided up. If this division becomes too marked and one partner gets left by the other, a great feeling of helplessness will ensue and a dread of exploring those neglected areas. Here is another vicious circle that needs to be broken. 'Old men', said Eliot, 'ought to be explorers'.[7] But so often they are not, and in the same poem he talks about their folly.

It is not so much that we have to force ourselves to adopt different attitudes, but that we need to be open and ready for the changes that will inevitably take place. If our souls are in tune with our bodies, we will become aware that the extremes of masculine and feminine, both biological and psychological, become less marked towards the end of life. A woman, when her children leave home, may take up a new career, a man become more inward-looking, more intuitive, perhaps more vulnerable, as he drops his macho image and loses his need to compete with his peers. A new grandfather held his daughter's first-born in his arms and experienced a tenderness he had never felt for his own children. To his surprise, he found himself wishing, very powerfully, that he had the female equipment to feed this child. A woman, married happily to a successful writer, identified entirely with her husband's fame. When he died, she felt empty until she discovered talents in herself that she had forgotten since her school days. These are illustrations of what Jung called the 'anima' and the 'animus', but also referred to as 'soul images' — the soul being the inner man, the reverse of what we show to the world. The man and woman, described above, each had to discover neglected aspects of themselves which they thought belonged exclusively to the opposite sex. Jung saw the task of later life as taking back these projections, by which he meant claiming these qualities as our own in order to become whole.

We cannot be reborn without a struggle, nor do we get rid of, or re-channel, our sexual energy at any easily recognizable age. If we are still actively sexual, or have the same longings, in our sixties, seventies and beyond, we will surely be happier in acknowledging that no transition is final. There are bound to be problems and some may be impossible to solve, but Jung makes the helpful suggestion that they may become 'outgrown'. 'Some higher or wider interest appeared on the patient's horizon, and through this broadening of his outlook the insoluble problem lost its urgency. It was not solved logically on its own terms, but faded out when confronted with a new and stronger life urge.'[8] Perhaps we need more patience.

As we approach the end of life, we may or may not experience a spiritual awakening. Not all of us are contemplative. Many of us seem content, especially if lucky enough to have grandchildren, to let another generation take over where we leave off, and live our lives vicariously through the young. Others want to learn a language, write a poem, paint a picture, try something entirely new.

Nowadays we are all encouraged to be 'creative' (it seems to be the 'in-word'), not least the old for whom art classes and creative writing groups abound. Many who left school early, rediscover talents that had gone into hibernation. The Second World War put a sudden stop to the schooling of many of today's pensioners. Working in a group together encourages the shy and is a way of sharing events in each other's lives which would otherwise have been lost. People want to record their memories. 'Getting it down is a way of affirming the continuity of life at the same time as relishing the mutations brought about by changing seasons or evolving circumstances. . . . It fixes things, it pins them down so that we possess the passing experience and later can recall it for our guidance and delight.'9 Here the author looks forward as well as back, using the past as a signpost for the future.

Through creativity we may find again our capacity for play. It is not for nothing that human childhood is both biologically and psychologically prolonged. 'To use his brain to the full,' wrote Anthony Storr, 'man had to linger in the childhood position.'10 'Second childhood' is not only a return but an awareness of the child we have always retained within us.

Children are full of curiosity, and are therefore discoverers. The very young and the very old often play imaginatively together. They have time for one another. The curiosity and playfulness of childhood is never quite expunged, merely crowded out by busy routines. Storr has this to say: 'Once established, curiosity may remain into extreme old age, and indeed, often appears to be the spice of life which "keeps things going."'11

The paradox of having time to think and do what we like, yet being confronted with the end of life, gives the necessary tension which so many writers agree provides the motive force for creativity. The old walk on a tightrope between the opposites of ending and beginning, and both are baffling. Life without tension is unimaginable and not conducive to any sort of exploration. There is a kind of restlessness, already hinted at earlier in this chapter, which is sometimes called 'divine discontent'; this is not a frenzied running after pleasure, but is more akin to St Augustine's famous saying: 'Thou has formed us for thyself and our hearts are restless till they find their rest in thee.'12

This kind of restlessness is a search for transcendence, which may have its origins in childhood play and is experienced by many in sexual orgasm; it is also experienced in nature and the arts and in every meaningful human relationship. The search goes on, although the goal may elude us to the end. The American gerontologist Robert Butler sees it as essential for creative living: 'I find great pressure to be inventive and re-inventive of different versions of self . . . a continuing life-long crisis is a sign of good health and the right to have such a crisis is one of the important rights to life. Human beings need the freedom to live with change, to invent and re-invent themselves a number of times throughout their lives.'[13]

If such reinvention of ourselves leads us back to childhood so that we learn again to be spontaneous and free from inhibition, let us never forget: 'Except ye become again as little children . . . ye shall not enter the Kingdom of heaven.'

Notes

1. W. B. Yeats, 'Sailing to Byzantium', *Collected Poems*, Macmillan 1937.
2. G. G. Marquez, *Love in the Time of Cholera*, Penguin 1989, pp. 340-1.
3. C. G. Jung, quoted in Samuels, Shorter and Plaut, *A Critical Dictionary of Jungian Analysis*, Routledge 1986, p. 30.
4. T. Mann, *Death in Venice*, Penguin 1971.
5. ibid., p. 47.
6. Abraham, Kocher and Goda, 'Psychoanalysis and Ageing', *International Review of Psychoanalysis*, vol. 7, 1980, pp. 147-55.
7. T. S. Eliot, 'East Coker' in *Four Quartets*, Faber 1979.
8. C. G. Jung, quoted in R. Wilhelm, *Secret of the Golden Flower: Chinese Book of Life*, Routledge 1962.
9. M. Harman, 'Celebrating Age Competition', organized by Chichester Diocesan Board for Social Responsibility 1987.
10. A. Storr, *The Dynamics of Creation*, Pelican 1976, p. 207.
11. ibid.
12. St Augustine, *Confessions*, Book 1, ch. 1, tr. F. J. Sheed, Sheed & Ward 1945, p. 1.
13. R. Butler, 'The Creative Life and Old Age', quoted in *Group Therapies for the Elderly*, Monograph 5, American Group Psychotherapy Association 1978, p. 219.

FOUR

Retirement

It is impossible to enjoy idling thoroughly
unless one has plenty of work to do.
Jerome K. Jerome

Freud's prescription for psychological health was to love and
to work. Playing and fantasy, in which one might include the
enjoyment of idling, were seen as a childish denial of reality.
It seems that, in Freud's psychology, the Protestant Work
Ethic comes across as strictly as it does in much religious
teaching.

At best, loving, working and playing are closely associated.
One loves one's work for its own sake, or one works for the
sake of a loved person, perhaps for the love of God.

If career and creativity coincide, work and play become
virtually indistinguishable. And it is this work/play that
gives life its meaning. But not everyone is so lucky. Work and
enjoyable living can be so separated that a large proportion
of the population spends its days watching the clock,
impatient for real life to begin. In neither of these cases is
retirement an undiminished blessing. The clock-watchers may
long for it without realizing how much the monotony of their
work saps the energy and dulls the will. There are few things
more tiring than being bored and, all too often, the pleasures
longed for after hours extend no further than food, drink,
television and bed. When retirement at last comes, the waiting
may have been too long. Treats are no longer treats when
they are available all the time, and the enthusiasm for
'something new' has died. To embark on a totally different
life needs careful preparation. Faced with what looks like an

41

empty future, perhaps a lot of us would 'rather bear those ills
we have, than fly to others that we know not of'.
There was, after all, some comfort in the daily routine, the
journey to and fro between home and workplace, the
undemanding chatter with one's mates and a shared
grumbling. If, on the other hand, life and work have become
inseparable, it may be even harder to hand over a precious
task to a young successor. Loss of position may seem like
losing one's life. The verbs 'to do' and 'to be' have taken on
the same meaning. Without 'doing', there is no 'being', no
identity left.

Retirement has no history. No tradition has yet attached
itself to its importance as a crucial stage of life, no
acknowledgement of what might be called its liminality —
that is, in more ordinary parlance, a threshold that needs to
be crossed. The word 'limen' is used psychologically to mean
the threshold of consciousness. We might say that retirement
is sub-liminal in that it has not yet made an impact on the
consciousness of the race. Without proper recognition,
retirement becomes a dangerous threshold. Some people
actually die as soon as they set foot over the sill. It has taken
us nearly a century to realize how much help might have been
given to them in their passage.

The history of retirement is barely a hundred years old.
From the time of Elizabeth I, who created the Poor Law, there
were, apart from the leisured classes, only workers and
paupers. If they were too crippled, mad or old to earn their
keep, paupers were sent to asylums. The able-bodied went to
workhouses and laboured till they dropped. There was little,
or no, state relief for those who risked staying in their own
homes, and it would not have occurred to older workers to
retire at any specified age. For as long as possible, they
avoided being categorized as paupers because of the stigma
attached to unproductive members of society. Although the
Poor Law was reformed — very imperfectly it seems — in
1834, and subjected to various later amendments, no scheme
of state pensions came into being till 1908, and it took
another twenty years or so to become fully established.
Pensions were given to wage-earners as rewards for their
services, rather than as an entitlement to relief in old age.

To quote Simone de Beauvoir, who describes how the old have been treated in various countries, both capitalist and socialist:

> The State sets the age at which a worker has the right to a retirement pension: this is also the age at which public and private employers dismiss their workers, and it is therefore that at which the individual passes from the active to the inactive category. When is this change to take place? What total must the contributions have reached? To decide upon this, society has to take two factors into account: its own interests and those of the pensioners.[1]

There are many political implications in this quotation, which it is not the purpose of this book to argue, but we cannot avoid seeing two reverse faces of retirement: (1) the philanthropic view that people should be relieved of the need to work in their old age and have earned the right to be supported; (2) the utilitarian view that the retired are a burden on society, consumers of its resources, with no productive value and therefore a liability. These alternatives sum up many of the paradoxes of growing old — those antitheses of respect versus contempt, gratitude versus unconcern, appreciation versus devaluation — all of which can cause so much conflict between the generations.

However relieved we may be that the shadow of the workhouse has long since vanished from sight, it is not easy to be unreservedly grateful to a state or institution that pulls the carpet from under our feet, according to a rule of someone else's making, and without any assessment of our capability (or lack of it) to go on contributing, or even being able to rise to higher positions.

The question of choice, to work or not to work, is seldom respected. Usually there is no individual who can be blamed for this, merely the rigidity of whatever system has entrapped us. At a time of recession and high unemployment, redundancy, disguised as an invitation to take early retirement, is a problem for mid-life and even youth, as much as for old age.

A friend's father was reaching the peak of his career when the civil service enforced the rule of retirement at sixty. The news was a shock as he realized that, instead of fulfilling what had seemed quite realistic ambitions for future promotion, he had achieved all that he would ever be allowed to achieve in what turned out to be his last posting. He had given little thought to his age, but now, as he approached his sixtieth birthday, he felt hurt and humiliated in seeing himself supposedly labelled as 'past his prime', only fit to be 'put out to grass'. There was, of course, no evidence that anyone saw him any differently from the way he was at fifty-nine; the rule had been implemented to give opportunities to younger men to climb the ladder, rather than a deliberate sacrifice of the old. Yet sacrificed he was on the altar of rigidity. There was no arguing with the rule, no special pleading. He had to go. Almost immediately, he developed various ailments and even had a minor operation. 'So they were right,' he said bitterly, and felt both depressed and anxious about the future. He had entered the service late, so he retired with a reduced pension. However, he was self-disciplined and not without inner resources. Some years later he embarked on a second career, but first he set himself the task of systematically reading the classics. Some of his closest friends (similarly unprepared for retirement) died, either of cancer or heart disease, soon after passing this dangerous threshold.

With the same sort of suddenness, an advertising executive in his mid-fifties was made redundant when a venture employing him abroad came to a sticky end. Back in England, he applied for several suitable jobs, but each time he found himself turned down because of his age. He was not confident enough to invest capital in founding a company of his own, which was what some of his ex-colleagues suggested. He had always preferred the position of second-in-command to that of boss, nor did he have quite the resourcefulness of the senior civil servant just described. After enjoying a few days eating out with his wife, walking the dog and reading detective stories, the holiday mood wore off. He had feelings of being adrift, dazed and unsure of his identity, and showed many of the symptoms now generally recognized in bereavement. Well-meaning friends suggested remedies but, to most of these, he responded very little. His wife was full of ideas but he turned them down, always with the answer that he was waiting for the right thing to turn up. She wondered how anything ever 'turned up' without going to look for it, and was bewildered by his apathy.

It was she who appealed to a managing lady at their local church, and soon word went round that her husband was prepared 'to do anything for the elderly'. Rather against his will, he found himself acting as chauffeur for two old couples who attended the Darby and Joan club a few miles away. He was kind and good humoured and they enjoyed his company on their drives, but this once-weekly job was hardly stimulating for him and was undertaken purely as a duty. As time went by, he started being invited to help with social activities at the club and soon made himself at home as the 'life and soul of the party'.

Something eventually did 'turn up' and became a prelude to more serious involvement in church affairs. His rector, who hardly knew him, suddenly telephoned and asked if he could help to produce a stewardship brochure. 'How did you know I was in advertising?' was the astonished reply. 'I didn't,' said the rector. 'I just had a hunch you might be the man I was looking for.' The brochure that resulted from the rector's hunch was professionally written and beautifully produced.

In the years that followed, our friend joined the PCC, followed by deanery and diocesan synods. He cared passionately about religion, but, with equal passion, he did not hesitate to criticize the Church. He argued his way through many meetings and often, though not always, made himself unpopular. He died before reaching old age, and clergy from all denominations were much in evidence at his funeral.

In this case, pastoral care seems to have been both given and received, but almost, it might seem, by mistake — unless, of course, one accepts the rector's hunch as divinely inspired. And, indeed, why not?

Some men take to retirement more easily. The following statement was written by someone who has always seemed to take life as it comes, with the minimum of fuss:

A lot of rubbish is written about retirement. When people — men and women — are approaching retirement age, they are being conditioned to believe that they must develop new interests and even that they need a course of instruction. . . . When I retired a few years ago, after many years in a job which I enjoyed and in which I took a pride, I had a feeling of guilt about not playing the bread-winner's part. . . . That lasted about a fortnight! After that I found increasingly that my time was occupied with jobs which might seem humble, but are really just as useful as many of the things one did in the course of earning a living.[2]

Here was someone who saw no need for help in crossing a threshold. He admitted to two worries, but they both proved groundless. The first was: 'How long would one remain fit and strong enough to lead a "normal" life? There are alarming tales of rapid mental and physical deterioration after giving up one's normal occupation.'[3] As it turned out, he lost a stone in weight during the first year and, relieved from the tensions of a demanding and sedentary job, found his health improved by digging and weeding the garden for two hours a day, always with the choice of timing his work according to the vicissitudes of the weather. His other worry was money: 'I have never been much of a one for keeping accounts, but I seem to have more money in my pocket available to spend than I ever had before. This is in spite of a substantial drop in income.'[4] This had to do with not needing to look smart and having the time to 'poke round the Oxfam shop', where, among other items, he found a pair of trousers for £4. He also enjoyed 'hanging about all day' at auction sales and snapping up bargains. And here is another quote: 'There are pounds and pounds to be saved shopping around in the market instead of the Saturday visit to the High Street shops. And have you ever known the pleasure of walking a mile or two to pick a free dish of sea spinach?'[5]

His only disappointment was falling asleep over books. He had planned to tackle novels, biographies and great works of philosophy, but his concentration faltered. Not only did the brain 'take the easy way out', but he remembered less and less of what he read.

A different story was told by an elderly lady who was determined to read the whole of Shakespeare before she went blind. After that, she would listen to all of Mozart. History does not relate whether she has succeeded! Or is she still at it?

Couples sometimes talk euphorically about feeling like 'kids out of school'. On the other hand, there have been quite a few grouses from wives about having to change their routines to accommodate stay-at-home husbands: 'I married him for life, not for lunch.' And this, from a man: 'No one can live with someone for twenty-four hours a day without some irritation. This is too much to expect even from a saint, and she isn't.' Men often miss the company of other men. Women sometimes miss their husbands' former colleagues, but usually retain friends of their own sex.

Women also retire from full-time jobs and may need as much help as their husbands in mourning the loss and adjusting to a new way of life. Simone de Beauvoir, writing more than twenty years ago, is sure that they adapt better than men:

> . . . life and work merge into one another. No decree from without cuts her activities short. . . . Apart from some exceptions, most women commit much less of themselves to their calling than men; and because of the number of young women who do not work, retirement does not automatically class them in a certain age-group. And they have a part to play in their homes and families that allows them to remain active and to retain their identity.[6] [One presumes she herself was one of the exceptions!]

Is any of this, one wonders, still true. For wives and mothers, there has always been a need to adapt. Even in these days of sharing housekeeping and, to a considerable extent, the mothering, it is women who need time off early in their working lives for pregnancy and childbirth. Preoccupation with babies has at times to be absolute and the working mother needs to learn a difficult balancing act between two very separate existences. Even the mood swings of the menstrual cycle accustom her to frequent changes in equilibrium. After the menopause she will probably achieve an inner stability, but not necessarily at the expense of her flexibility. It does seem that retired women easily pick up outside activities — some paid, some voluntary — and a lot of their chosen work involves caring for people in need. More women than men take counselling courses, become Samaritans, visit the sick and housebound, volunteer for 'meals on wheels' — to name but a few of the possibilities open to them.

Retirement for single women brings a greater problem of loneliness. The decisive break at sixty, with only a perfunctory office party as rite of passage, followed by that return to an empty flat, can feel like the beginning of dying. One hopes that someone, whether friend or pastoral worker, will recognize this as bereavement. And yet, even the loneliest of women surprise us in due time. How often one hears the words 'I've never been busier in my life!'

And what about the clergy? Priests of course never retire, but vicars do — as do bishops and other church dignitaries. They relinquish jobs, but not their vocations. It is noticeable that they do not retire, even from these jobs, as early as the average layman. A century ago, vicars stayed on in their parishes until they died or became so incapable that they ended their days in the workhouse or, if they were lucky, some more charitable institution. The Clergy Pensions Board came into being at much the same time as the establishment of state pensions, so the history was much the same as for lay people, though stipends were notoriously low and there was often little chance of saving enough to buy one's own house.

Today, most incumbents retire before seventy, though they may still find it hard to let go of a ministry that has been happy and fulfilling. Some may overstay their welcome, but few die in harness. Others are relieved to drop responsibilities and take on more limited roles. On retirement, the options seem to be: (1) to stay at home (if one has one) and call it a day, (2) to move to a chosen area and into a house one can afford, then wait to be invited to help in a local parish, (3) to advertise for part-time ministry in return for accommodation. The trouble with option (3) is its impermanence: no home of one's own after finally giving up all work.

Opportunities for ministry will depend on where the retired priest decides to settle. It may be just as well that soaring prices make the south coast (the 'Costa Geriatrica') less attractive than formerly. Thirty years ago, there were said to be more retired clergy living in and around Bournemouth than in the Peterborough diocese as a whole. All in all, there seem to be more retired than parochial clergy, a fact that has compelled the Church Commissioners to direct their main inherited resources to clergy pensions.

However eager the retiring priest may be to offer his services, not all incumbents welcome them. A senior, well-known, talented priest can pose quite a threat to the 'kingship' of a young vicar. By the same token, the retired priest himself needs enough inner security to shun the limelight and be prepared to take second place.

A year before his own retirement as Archbishop of Canterbury, Robert Runcie, addressing the Retired Clergy Association, quoted from Christopher Bryant's book, *The River Within*: 'One of the tasks of later life, more especially for the years of retirement, is to look back at the joys and sorrows, the successes and failures, the unresolved problems and the unfinished tasks of the past; *to look back in order to let go*.'[7]

In one of his sermons, Cuthbert Bardsley, former Bishop of Coventry, reflected on retirement as a time for making fresh contact with God and seeing him in a new light: 'It is important to take time in our old age to be still, so that we can become more aware of the God who makes Himself known in quietness.' He bids us leave behind 'the busy manuals of prayer'. 'In the prayer of old age we shall learn to float on the all pervasive, all available strength and love of God. We shall learn to relax and to listen to the still small voice and to rely upon it.'[8] He too was speaking to retired clergy, but his message was for all of us as we grow older and less busy. If the clergy can learn to 'float', as he suggests, on God's love, how much better equipped they will be to give pastoral help to a wide variety of men and women who are using periods of inactivity, as they get older, to make more of their prayer life — 'to do less and *be* more holy'.

This 'floating' and 'letting go' is, in its quiet way, a reminder of the Hindu sannyasin who, solicitous for their spiritual welfare, set aside the last years of their life to practise detachment from the world — sometimes actually as mendicants with begging bowls, free from all ties of wealth or family. Some such loosening from worldly concerns (even if more metaphorically) could well be seen as the 'vocation' of old age.

In a later chapter, we shall examine how the ageing process affects religious orders, whose members grow old like the rest of us, but who do not usually think in terms of retirement. As we shall see, there is no defined threshold, nor, in most cases, a rigid age limit at which familiar activities must stop. Monks and nuns often have what, in secular terms, we would call careers, but they are not brought up to be career-minded. As human beings, they will probably during their working lives have ambitions for personal success, but if getting on in the rat race was what mattered they would not have chosen religious communities as their arenas. The overriding ambition for any religious must surely be to attain the Kingdom of Heaven. However, as with the clergy, jobs do come to an end and adjustment to a slower rhythm of activity is not necessarily smooth.

The Roman Catholic Association of Senior Religious (ASR) was founded in 1974 and has made a study of the needs of older 'retired' members of religious houses. Looking through the foundation statutes of these houses and their hundreds of directives, these needs were found to be largely ignored. Here is one of very few references: 'Each sister, aware that retirement is a time for personal growth and continual participation in the life and mission of the community, will prepare herself for this period, and the community will assist her in this preparation.' No mention is made of how she is to be assisted.

Before the ASR was officially launched, a questionnaire was devised to discover the views of those sisters who were about to 'retire'. They were asked such questions as what did they mean by 'personal growth', what continuing participation could they look forward to in the life and mission of the community, and what preparation — such as courses or conferences — would be appreciated.

The findings gave the ASR definite objectives to explore in order to develop the contribution of the older religious to the apostolic mission of the Church. Men's orders and Church of England orders are now also represented.

In 1984 the ASR undertook a survey on second 'apostolates' — or, in lay language, retirement jobs — being done by older sisters. There is now a focus on personal choice and treating each sister as an individual with her own contribution, whether in the educational field or in pastoral care and social ministry. Personal fulfilment no longer seems a bar to the Kingdom of Heaven, but perhaps something more like an open door.

One rather unique community belongs to this chapter rather than later in the book. This is because retirement is its essential feature, affecting each member from the moment of entry until her departure. As a subject for this book, it hardly qualifies. A community whose inmates retire from membership is always a young community, for whom care of the old and helpless is never a problem. St Julian's was founded to provide rest and refreshment for missionaries on furlough, but has now become a place of sanctuary for tired workers in all sorts of professions — for anyone, in fact, who needs a breathing space in which to be looked after for a few days instead of endlessly caring for other people. The house is not intended as a rest home for the old, although a few retired friends (who were frequent visitors during their years of full-time employment) are still welcomed for short stays in their later years.

Tempting as it is to describe in detail this 'evolving' community, bound by no rule (only loyalty to one another and their common cause), all that is relevant here is the fact that each member, at some unspecified time in her mid-sixties, does in fact leave — not just her job, but the house itself.

The attitude is best explained by one of the members:

I believe that the fact that each one of us will eventually retire subtly and significantly affects our daily life together

— it provides a healthy counterbalance against an almost inevitable pull towards becoming institutionalized and too dependent on the group. It seems to affirm part of our ethos, that the effect of our life in the Community should be to strengthen and deepen the inner being of each of us, so that we move on to another stage in our life's journey at the appropriate time. And that right time is very much for individual members to discover for themselves — most have known fairly clearly when they felt the right time approaching for a fresh pace and pattern of life. They have discovered that there is work to be done in retirement and old age which is significantly different from that asked during the years in Community.[9]

These words come from a still active member. Another, who has long since made the break, said that living without the assurance of being looked after in one's old age meant one had to make one's own plans, though she admitted that she had never planned far ahead. She saw herself as adventurous and taking opportunities as they arose. When she joined St Julian's, she worked on the community farm, and then was one of four members who opened a house in Kenya. When both that house and the farm in Sussex were given up, she quite looked forward to her retirement. She bought her own country cottage (personal money is kept and put aside for when it is needed) and started thinking about whether to join the WVS or Meals on Wheels. In the end she did neither. She wanted time to think about herself and come to terms with the past. Sometimes she wondered if she was being useless, but that phase seems to have passed. She realizes that she has been given a gift — the ability to make friends: 'A lot of people come and see me and we talk.' She is still in touch with St Julian's and all the friends she made in her community days, but does not regret leaving. Being with people is important, but so perhaps is solitude.

As we have seen, individual attitudes to retirement are enormously variable. If people are self-sufficient enough to want to be left alone to 'get on with it', their privacy needs to be respected. Nevertheless, none of us can realistically envisage beforehand exactly what feelings of loss and diminishment may be experienced when that important threshold has to be crossed. This is true of many of life's transitions. Earlier in this century, most women gave up paid work on marriage. After the initial excitement of wedding and honeymoon, there could be a sudden shock of loneliness on being left in the house for long hours to cook and iron shirts for husbands who continued to live their lives as before, with the bonus of being greeted with a kiss and a cooked meal at the end of the day. Having, they thought, attained their hearts' desires, these women were quite unprepared for such 'post-wedding blues'. Nowadays, this feeling is more likely to hit wives when they have babies, who, however delightful, are not much good at making conversation!

It is the unsuspected shock that needs to be guarded against. Not unlike first-time mothers, the newly retired may hide their feelings of loss under masks of pride and assure all visitors that their armchairs, gardens and the freedom to potter are a blissful escape from years of drudgery. Any other feelings may be hidden, even from themselves. It is important not to be intrusive in this situation and full of unasked-for questions. All one can do is to watch and wait in case — or until — help is more obviously needed.

Even in the case of those who have never thought ahead and planned for themselves, others can get busy planning for them. Pre-retirement courses are now on offer, both in industry and some of the professions, and employers are often willing to give their staff time off to attend them. Some firms foot the bill; others expect employees to pay for themselves. There is still a dearth of courses available and only a small percentage of eligible candidates takes advantage of them. But, increasingly, there is seen to be a need to prepare for this important transition.

The WEA run a three-day course with a strong practical emphasis. A whole day is spent on financial matters. This has been nicknamed the 'Death Day', as much of it is taken up with the mechanics of bereavement, funeral arrangements, insurances and bequests. At least 30 per cent of those attending have been found not to have made wills. A good half have never discussed retirement with their spouses. Another day concentrates on health, diet and exercise. Lastly, there will be discussion on the all-important topic of relationships, especially the effect of retirement on married couples, some of whom come on the course together. All walks of life are represented, from dustmen to top executives. The WEA are also now giving attention to redundancy courses, where much stronger feelings of loss and frustration are likely to be expressed.

Pre-retirement seminars, consisting of two morning sessions, are being held at the United Nations Centre in Vienna and probably in other related organizations. Detailed advice is given on pensions, banking, tax, form-filling, health and life insurance, and choices, both about how to take out one's pension and about where to live, with a warning not to leave major decisions till the last minute. The second session is about personal adjustment, and the one described to us was taken by a Jungian analyst. He called retirement a 'Third Life', which, with luck, could last another twenty or thirty years, so it ought to be sensibly planned and enjoyed. 'It is an entering in and not a shutting out.'[10]

When retirement courses were first planned, important issues were pensions, housing and use of leisure. Only gradually did the psychological problems emerge. Research reveals that two years before retiring people tend to worry about money, whereas two years after the crucial date they are more concerned with the meaning of life.

The Pre-Retirement Association of Great Britain and Northern Ireland now runs training courses for course providers. These may be laid on by local retirement associations or adult education colleges. Many dioceses provide courses for clergy and their wives, and the Christian Council on Ageing runs them for both clergy and lay people.

Elizabeth Harbottle, Chairman of the Christian Council on Ageing, describes the spiritual crisis of retirement as an 'Exodus' experience:

It is a desert place; a place to develop spiritual strength, a place for life review and discovery of resources, skills and experiences built up over a life-time; it is a place of suffering, of facing regrets of the past, failures and missed opportunities, a time to feel the pointlessness of the journey so far or to fear the traumas that may lie ahead. The apparently empty desert, seemingly useless and impractical like prayer, can, like prayer, be the most creative and fruitful. It is a watershed, a time to try out new things and shed others. It is a time to get to know oneself better. . . . Ageing is a process which takes a whole life-time, this major transition cannot be achieved in a matter of days. As one cannot live the afternoon of life without having experienced the morning, so the morning will affect the nature of the afternoon, yet the afternoon cannot be lived as if it were the morning. Jung: 'the afternoon of life must have a significance of its own and cannot be merely an appendage of life's morning'.[11]

Suggestions for people who want to make their journey in solitude include giving oneself time to write a journal or brief autobiography, attending to one's dreams, writing one's obituary and going on a silent or Ignatian retreat.

Elizabeth Harbottle recommends that organized courses should take five or six days, spread over many weeks, and should cover the whole range of human activity: from practical management of finance to one's personal philosophy of life.

It has been suggested that for any pre-retirement course to be of value, maximum participation of all involved is necessary. Organizers should be prepared to keep their programmes flexible to allow for exploration by group members.

In discussing the management of money in retirement, a specifically Christian course might try to relate it to concepts of hope and providence and to Christian stewardship. A day on health would go beyond mere physical fitness (based on staying younger longer) to make links with emotional and spiritual health in later life. The subject of leisure opportunities would lead to discussion on the meaning of work in Christian life, the relationship between role and person, the meaning of status, of power and loss of power, and the nature of a Christian person's identity.

Courses of this kind evolve slowly and the nature of each will depend on the individual journey of every participant. Exciting discoveries may be made, not all of them without pain. With full participation from each member, a lot of hard work will be done — and perhaps also a certain amount of play. If there is a time for everything under the sun, both work and idling may come to be enjoyed thoroughly.

Finally, what about a Christian 'rite of passage' to initiate us into this second (or some people seem to be saying 'third') life of retirement? Our other important transitions in life are marked by baptism, confirmation, first communion, marriage and, for some, ordination. In the old days, there was a special rite after childbirth called 'The Churching of Women'. The only other acknowledged rite is the last of all: the funeral.

The omission of any special rite for retirement obviously has to do with history, as explained at the beginning of this chapter. Now that retirement has come to stay, its important liminality needs recognition, not least by the Church. In devising an acceptable retirement service, there could be an emphasis on 'letting go', but also on 'going forth' to encounter new adventures and challenges — with, one hopes, full support of friends and colleagues, in, as we used to say, 'this congregation here present'.

Notes

1. S. de Beauvoir, *Old Age*, Penguin 1977, p. 252.
2. 'Retirement is Nothing to be Scared of' (signed J.R.W.), *Chichester Diocesan News*, August 1981.
3. ibid.
4. ibid.
5. ibid.
6. de Beauvoir, *Old Age*, p. 294.
7. C. Bryant, *The River Within*, Darton, Longman & Todd 1978.
8. C. Bardsley, 'Reflections of an Old Man', Address to Retired Clergy Association 1985.

9. A. R. Day, 'St Julians 1941–1986. Reflections upon an Evolving Religious Community' (a talk given to the Guild of Pastoral Psychology 1986).
10. M. Lewis, 'The Door is Opening not Shutting', VIC Pre-Retirement Seminars, *AIEA Staff News* 1984.
11. E. Harbottle, unpublished material.

FIVE

Endings

―――――

What we call the beginning is often the end,
And to make an end is to make a beginning.
The end is where we start from.

T. S. Eliot, 'Little Gidding'

We start by plunging in, or being pushed out. In the act of being born, we leave behind us the closest human relationship we ever have and go forth from the safe containment of the womb into an enormous, unknown world. For the mother too there is an ending, which is bound to be a mixture of relief, anxiety and anticipation. She has the advantage of knowing something about what she and her baby can expect of each other, but, as the one who knows, she is also the one responsible for all the shocks and changes of their future interactions. For both mother and baby there has to be an expulsion from the Garden of Eden. In becoming conscious — and especially in becoming conscious of ourselves as individuals — we all have to eat from the tree of knowledge and learn the difference between good and evil, closeness and separation. From birth to old age, human life is a series of endings and beginnings. There may be nostalgia and mourning, and there are ways of using these feelings creatively, but we can never put the clock back and retrieve what we have lost.

Without loss there can be no advance. Jung, in his middle age, looked back on his childhood as blissful, exciting and dangerous. He said of it: 'the pull of that other world was so strong that I had to tear myself violently from the spot in order not to lose hold of my future'.[1]

In writing about the losses of old age, one keeps

58

remembering the earlier losses, the difficult endings and, perhaps, even more complicated beginnings, that confront us at every stage. We all have to be weaned. We have to get out of bed and walk. We have to go to school. As we let go of infancy, we may have to allow for a younger brother or sister to become the centre of our parents' attention, and even the youngest must learn to share Mother's love with such rivals as, for instance, Father. We start, if we are reasonably lucky, by feeling as omnipotent as kings and queens, but we soon have to abdicate. Some get pushed off the throne before they are ready and may, in consequence, remain insecure for the rest of their lives. How we cope with early upheavals sets the pattern for future experience. We have probably all been advised at some time to finish one task before starting another, but we may not have been helped to do so during the early transitions of life.

Some endings are universal and we accept and predict them, like the tides or the year's seasons, as part of the ebb and flow of existence. But sometimes nature itself seems unnatural. Buds get frost-bitten and storms shorten the time of blossoming. There may be earthquakes and tidal waves. Death often happens out of season. And so it is with human beings. There are bound to be obstacles, whether early or late, to hinder self-fulfilment. Some are obviously external, but others remain hidden. Often those who cannot settle into a serene old age have experienced no serenity as children. So life repeats the pattern of the beginning. Sometimes people can be helped to rearrange their patterns, but only if they can first become aware of the repetitions. Often there may be a need to mourn, even years afterwards, for a loss that was ignored when it happened. Unresolved grief tends to be very tenacious, even if the cause has been forgotten.

If parents separate when their children are very young, all too often they are so taken up with their own trauma that the children's pain goes almost unrecognized. Even if 'civilized' arrangements are made for seeing 'Daddy' every weekend, it must always be bewildering to a child, longing for a lost togetherness, to discover that adults, in not making up their quarrels, are failing to practise what they preach. It is the children who, in the ups and downs of their peer-group friendships, seem better able to manage forgiveness and reconciliation. If a parent moves away altogether, sometimes the children are not told at all: 'Why did Mummy cry so much? He often went away on business. She told us he would soon be home. But she went on crying and he never came back.'

A child who grows up with secrets is likely to be a distrustful adult. Many quite old people still feel deprived of parental care and go on helplessly looking for a saviour to put things right. Those whose fathers let them down may have a lot of difficulty with religious faith and particularly in accepting God as 'Father'.

Sometimes the biggest secret of all is death. Although attitudes are beginning to change, attempts to protect children from a reality that is hard to explain are likely to heighten rather than diminish the inevitable suffering.

One little girl was brought up without being told that she had an identical twin who died at birth. Always, she had an undefined feeling of something missing. When at last she was considered old enough to have her questions answered, she found the place where she imagined her twin to have been buried and got in the habit of taking flowers to the grave. She was trying, ritualistically, to acknowledge an ending. But this was not allowed. Her older sister told her the unpalatable truth that there was no grave to visit. Stillbirth in those days was treated like miscarriage, and her twin turned into a non-person.

Not everyone encounters death when very young, but we all experience a succession of partial deaths. Moving house is recognized these days as one of life's big traumas. As adults, we usually have some degree of choice. Children are at the mercy of parental necessity — or what sometimes looks like parental whim — and they deserve proper explanations, along with the recognition that it is sad, for instance, to leave a school where work was going well and one had made a lot of friends. Each transition should have its appropriate mourning.

One child, who was moved round the world from infancy onwards, experienced her life as a series of unrelated pictures.

At the age of four, when about to return to England on leave, her older sister tested her memory, describing their grandparents and their London home. When she got to England, she found herself dimly remembering and recognizing. This helped to give her some sense of continuity. This child grew up with a dread of upheavals and a strong fear of death, which seemed like falling over the edge of the world. Being sent to boarding school at an early age, while giving some of the necessary continuity, also reinforced the stops and starts that had so characterized the first years of her life. She had a continuing difficulty in letting go of people and places, and could only move on to new beginnings after prolonged mourning of the past. Recognizing this need in herself, and having it recognized by others, gradually lessened her homesickness and she became able to welcome, rather than dread, some of the surprises of the present.

We are often advised to live in the here and now, as the only reality. Yet that 'now' that we are experiencing has been shaped by what preceded it and will affect the future. Both past and future can take us by surprise.

Friends who drift apart may hardly recognize each other after a lapse of years. Reunions, much looked forward to, sometimes prove disappointing. Even the reminiscences do not always fit. We cling to our own version, but memory is selective and we all have different stories. Faced with variations, we may argue, or be lucky enough to find ourselves laughing at the discrepancies. Sometimes, like picking up an old book, we can carry on friendships from where we left them off, but there is always the risk of disillusionment. It can be quite a shock to come across a once glamorous lover and then, perhaps, to thank God for a lucky escape. We tend to forget that, for each of the protagonists, there has been a parting of the ways. If we had shared our stories and changed together through the years, then perhaps, after all, we might have continued to the end. There is no knowing what might have been and it is obviously wise to shun the useless pursuit of 'if only . . .'.

Many endings are imperceptible. There is not often an announcement: 'This is my last game of golf', or 'I'll never go abroad again', but, unconsciously, this fact may have been registered. Nature works unobtrusively and the ageing person begins saying 'No' to invitations that would earlier have been impossible to resist. Our longings change and no one notices, least of all ourselves.

When it comes to travel, many of today's OAPs are being given undreamed-of opportunities to see the world. Others feel privileged to have lived before the package tour: to have seen Athens before pollution, or Mount Hymettus turning an astonishing purple before sunset, the islands deserted. As for the Costa del Sol — one sixty-five-year-old, on being shown a photograph of an inland Spanish village, white-washed in the sun, exclaimed, 'It's just like Torremolinos.' 'When did you last go there?' 'Let me see — it must have been 1935.' She was advised never to return.

Those who carry into old age photographic memories of childhood scenes have also managed, for most of their lives, to feel again the emotions that accompanied the pictures. Yet eventually these feelings lose their freshness and may be remembered as if belonging to someone else. Sometimes the pictures in our minds become less colourful, fading like old photographs. We may be sad and also perhaps a little relieved at this detachment from strong emotion, but we will probably have sudden reminders. For one old lady, the smell of marigolds brought back the wonder of hot summers and long hours of play as well as painful teasing by an older brother. Tunes, once danced to, can stir up long-forgotten feelings — a mixture perhaps of joy, excitement or embarrassment. Children, surrounded by quite new and different toys from ours, may surprise us by wanting the same stories or asking the sort of questions that worried us long ago. Then, a minute later, they remove themselves to a world of electronics and computers and leave us far behind.

Getting old may feel like acting in a play where the rest of the cast is new and most of the props have changed. There is something familiar about the plot, but we have smaller parts to play, with a lot of time waiting in the wings before making a final bow. For many people, the worst fear is to be 'unwept, unhonoured and unsung', but serenity comes through managing not to mind.

And then there is that habit of scanning the newspapers — no longer for marriages and births, but for deaths and obituaries. As we get into our sixties and beyond, our friends begin to disappear, sometimes at an alarming rate, and bits of ourselves go missing with them.

Long before we die, many of us face very obvious partial deaths, in that we lose physical functions, movement, sight, or hearing. We may even have to surrender parts of our bodies, such as limbs or internal organs. Some of these losses are visible and evoke other people's sympathy. Others are unseen. For women, a hysterectomy marks a very definite end of female functioning. Mastectomy can also symbolize a death of femininity. It is all too visible to the sufferer, as also to her husband, but is sometimes masked from the world with an uncomfortable prothesis that may feel like a lump of dead flesh. One such sufferer wrote in her diary: 'They tell me I'm lucky. After all, it might have been worse. It was only a spare part. But I've lost a bit of *me* and I don't feel complete without it.' Her husband assured her that he loved her as much as ever and she believed him, though sometimes she felt vain in minding so much when he appeared to take it in his stride, and she would have liked him to do some mourning with her.

Many lose marriages. Divorce differs from widowhood in that the memories are spoiled. Others keep their partners, but can no longer communicate with them. The onset of Alzheimer's disease means watching a slow death. At first the symptoms are subtle and the person closest — wife or husband — is merely puzzled or surprised at feeling irritation and a gradual non-recognition of that familiar companion. A painful stage is when the sufferer is aware of the changes but feels powerless to stop things getting worse. And yet the partner is bound to welcome any lucidity that remains. The support of friends is all important. In one case, the illness lasted several years, but the sufferer's wife kept life going as normally as she could for as long as possible. Conversation with him had stopped making sense, and yet he was as gentle and courteous as he had always been, and seemed to charm his many helpers into continuing to include him in what went on and even gently laughing with (not at) him. One evening, he greeted a guest by taking her coat and letting it fall to the ground. She quickly picked it up and thanked him with a smile. His funeral was a celebration of a successful life and an exceptionally happy marriage; and the years of anguish soon fell into their rightful place as only a very small part of the whole. It was that whole his widow mourned, as did all his friends.

Losing what we love, nostalgia for a lost paradise, attempts to hang on to 'a joy as it flies' — all these experiences are part of the movement of life. Living 'happily ever after' would be impossibly static, and more like death than life. As we grow older, both loss and expectation of loss will increase, but some kind of bereavement, as we have seen, is already familiar and the many transitions of growing up involve an acknowledged renunciation of the past before we can move on to the next stage.

Freud wrote a famous paper on 'Mourning and Melancholia', in which he tried to separate the two.[2] Other authors have distinguished between 'normal' and 'pathological' mourning, usually according to how long it takes to 'get over' the loss. 'Getting over' seems an unfortunate phrase, suggesting denial. 'Working through' is perhaps more appropriate. Freud describes 'detaching the libido bit by bit', a setting free of trapped energy to find a new direction. He sees this as a struggle.

A child's first encounter with death is often the loss of a pet animal. This may be felt more intensely than the death of a human being, the favourite dog or cat having been a much fondled companion with whom more has been shared than with an ageing relative. But only limited grieving is expected. No ceremony surrounds the end, which may be a rushed visit to the vet and an act of what seems like murder. Deathbeds are avoided, funerals unlikely. The pet may be quickly replaced. One child who lost her dog soon after the death of her father admitted that she had grieved most for the dog, but 'the feeling didn't last so long'. Mourning for her father came later. Growing up as an only child in a one-parent family, she became more and more aware of a hole that could not be filled.

Not being present at the deathbed or funeral, having nowhere to visit, no memorial, all these absences can distort reality. One survivor of a pair of friends had recurrent dreams in which she searched for the girl who had died, in order to finish a conversation or make up a quarrel. Eventually realization broke through one of these dreams. 'I'm fifty,' she found herself saying, 'and that girl of twenty-five doesn't exist.' Later she went to look for the actual grave. After finding the place and reading the inscription, the recurring dreams stopped. It had taken more than twenty-five years to let go of her friend. This story may well sound 'pathological', yet, despite the length of time needed to round off an unfinished relationship, the survivor's life was not crippled. She married and easily made new friends. Her mourning was unconscious and confined to her dreams.

Not infrequently there is an accompaniment of guilt. 'Why should I be the one to live on?' This is especially true for survivors of the holocaust, who somehow found the strength to live through horrific experiences. Powerless to help their friends, they could only try to save themselves and had to watch others die. No wonder their nightmares persist, not only for them but for their children, many of whom have continued to feel guilty about being alive when so many died. Yet there were some survivors who managed to adjust surprisingly well and make friends in a new environment and, despite the outrage that they had to suffer, could feel a compensatory pride, gratitude or even a sense of rebirth. One might hazard a guess that these were the ones who had come from secure homes, and had thus been better able to re-create something that they had once enjoyed.

Each person's response to loss is highly individual and depends, as we have already seen, on traumas encountered early in life. We have mentioned Freud's distinction between mourning and melancholia. 'In mourning it is the world which has become poor and empty; in melancholia it is the ego itself.'[3] Perhaps this differentiation is too clear-cut. There is some melancholia in all of us, enough to give even so-called 'normal' mourning a touch of pathology. Who is to say, for instance, how long the tears, or the yearning, should last? In the case of the childhood friend, mentioned above, the survivor appeared to shake off her grief easily. Her mourning went underground, emerging only in dreams. She needed, in full consciousness, to let go of that part of her 'self' that was still attached to her friend. She needed to free herself from that particular bit of her past in order to mature.

A feeling of emptiness, both of the world and oneself, is likely to be extreme when it comes to the death of a marriage partner of many years standing. To be 'one flesh' involves a complete mutual belonging, conscious, unconscious, physical and spiritual. The newly bereaved live for a time in a limbo state. Some describe it as 'floating in space'. Separation, though never complete, may be on the way when the survivor can at last begin saying 'I' instead of 'we' and allow for change in a world that the partner will never share.

One of the hardest bereavements is a mother's loss of her child. Here, fate has turned the natural order upside down. No wonder she cries out, 'It should have been me.' If she can turn her anger against God, this seems the natural and appropriate thing to do. It may even be an act of faith: faith in a God who can bear the full force of that anger without being destroyed. And, if anyone is to blame, surely *he* is!

When someone in the family dies, the grief most likely to be recognized is that of the spouse. Certainly this should never be underestimated and, for most of us, being widowed is the worst that ever happens to us. But a son or daughter, parent, even (in one case that comes to mind) a mother-in-law — each has a special bereavement to go through, sometimes without much acknowledgement or consolation. Our emphasis in this book is on the older generation, but one cannot stress too much that all of us are continually ageing and that bereavement, even in youth, pushes us unexpectedly into the future. In the same way, sudden illness gives a foretaste of an old age for which the young are ill-prepared. Whereas a parent losing a child declares, 'It should have been me', a young person who is facing unexpected bereavement or disability comes up with the outraged question, 'Why me?'

Mourning, at any age, has to be seen as a task to be accomplished, a movement towards maturity and new experience. But growing pains hurt and a lot of time is needed. No one should prophesy an arbitrary period, such as two years, when such mourning should be completed. Everyone's time-scale is different. But the task of mourning is obviously very necessary. If blocked at the time of loss, it will merely be delayed, and too many prescriptions for tranquillizers, though comforting when the misery is acute, may result only in the postponement of necessary suffering. Elisabeth Kübler-Ross has pioneered the naming of different stages in the mourning process that are likely to be experienced. Following her suggestions, most books on bereavement present us with a scheme such as the following: (1) numbness, (2) searching, (3) despair, (4) integration. There are many variations, but in all of them importance is given to accepting the loss, experiencing the pain, and adjusting to an environment in which the deceased is missing, so that eventually there can be a reinvestment of energy (Freud's libido) in new relationships. Those who care for the bereaved have found these stages helpful, but it would be a mistake to have a rigid expectation of an orderly timetable in which each stage follows the other in succession.

For those who actually suffer the loss, the process tends to be muddled and there can be violent alternations of opposite feelings. Integration may even come near the beginning, in so far as one feels a sense of completeness about the dead person's life and a realization that what has been given cannot be taken away. This will probably be reinforced by eulogies at the funeral and letters of condolence. Answering these letters is usually a welcome task rather than a chore. As well as being simply something to do, it fulfils a strong wish to go on thinking about the dead person and share one's thoughts with others. Shock can sometimes even give way to elation. Only gradually, as the comforters withdraw, does the emptiness yawn and the first shock repeats itself again and again, with the realization that solitude has come to stay. How often the would-be comforters get their timing wrong. If only they would listen and allow the mourners to work through their grief in their own time, for however long it takes, and, above all, refrain from changing the subject in the mistaken belief that repeating the same sentiments is morbid and should be discouraged. Often the bereaved person *does* change the subject, not for her own sake but out of compassion for the listener's fear of intimacy. We are conditioned to feel that tears and displays of emotion are embarrassing.

Murray Parkes, in his otherwise excellent book on bereavement, tells us not to be worried by what he calls 'hallucinations', assuring us that they will not trouble us for long.[4] He does not seem to realize that, far from being threatening, these intimations of a loved person's presence can be moments of great joy. Sometimes the awareness is so strong that we long for more, but usually the experience is fleeting and diminishes as the reality of the loss gets accepted, disappearing altogether when the necessary separation is accomplished.

It is hard to allow the world to change, unshared by a much-loved partner, but eventually one has to let go. Few people now would consider Queen Victoria's protracted mourning to be healthy, and perhaps Dickens's description of Miss Haversham's yellowing bridal dress is a warning to all who are tempted to cling to a vanished past. In fact, those pasts that are clung to most tenaciously may be no more than fantasies of perfection. A good reality is likely to be internalized as a continuing source of inspiration.

Internalization is a technical word, meaning (most especially in this context) that we are able to absorb what we have been given by other people and make it our own. Old age would be boring, as well as sad, if we had not kept alive inside us the affection and help of parents, friends and lovers. We may not agree with all their opinions, nor have we necessarily taken their advice. We have had to sift the wheat from the chaff in order to become unique individuals. We may even continue internal arguments with the dead. Often we wish we had treated them better. At best, we try and look at our lives together as making a pattern, even if some odds and ends are tangled or still straggle; and perhaps we hope, with humility and gratitude, that on the whole we did our best, even if hindsight now shows us what might have been better. Always there will be something to mourn, but eventually that too has to come to an end — and it is not for officious outside helpers to tell us when that ending will come about. Like all clichés, there is truth in the saying that time heals. With no effort, or even wish on our part, we cannot avoid change. Yesterday becomes misty and today's reality takes over. There will be moments of longing for the past and the mixed blessing of nostalgia, which is painful as well as precious. But we can never be conscious of everything at once, and right up till the end of our lives each new day is another move and brings some surprise, however small.

Eventually there may be some awareness of a time of preparation even though this preparation is impossible to define. Life comes full circle and death is like birth. Once more we plunge into the unknown: 'In my end is my beginning.'

Notes

1. C. G. Jung, *Memories, Dreams and Reflections*, Collins/Routledge 1963, p. 36.
2. S. Freud, 'Mourning and Melancholia', in *On Metapsychology*, vol 11, Pelican 1917, p. 266.
3. ibid.
4. C. M. Parkes, *Bereavement*, Pelican 1972.

SIX

Signposts from Religious Communities

This, then, is the good zeal, which monks should foster with fervent love: they should each try to be the first to show respect to the other.

The Rule of St Benedict

Are religious communities on their way out? Do they have any wisdom to impart to the inhabitants of what is contrastingly referred to as 'the world'? In fact, not only is the spiritual life of the conventual world alive and well, but religious communities also play a specific role in caring for the elderly and helping each one of us to face our ageing as best we can.

Monasteries and convents impinge so little on our secular society that they tend to be viewed with a vague distaste. They are often seen as places of escape, where inmates have opted out of 'real life' and, for no obvious purpose, adopted a strange garb and even stranger customs. Apart from an invisible life of prayer, we may decide that their *real* work would be carried on a good deal better by paid professionals.

There are many jokes about the diminishment of once thriving communities, and most of these originate from inside them. One nun says to another, 'When you have only three novices, you feel a fool lining them up two by two.' This wry humour helps to soften the reality of deserted corridors that once echoed with the footsteps of young men and women preparing for the religious life.

The monastic population reflects the general ageing of our society. When the average age is sixty-plus, young people are understandably reluctant to test a possible vocation. 'Several have "looked" — liked what they saw, but . . .' This comment came from a community reduced to thirteen, aged between sixty and ninety-one, who were just about managing their activities with extra help from a maintenance man and a gardener (both pensioners), a fourteen-year-old schoolboy who polished the floor once a week, plus a bit of voluntary assistance from associates.

Traditionally, religious orders have relied on the young as their source of recruitment and renewal. In the Roman Catholic Church, many families used to feel duty-bound to head a daughter towards a convent and a son towards the priesthood. This tradition, with fewer practising Catholics and smaller families, is fast disappearing. The mystique seems to have gone out of the religious life. Priests and nuns must now prove themselves as human beings, with no hiding behind their collars or distinctive clothes. Neither the habit, nor their words, are automatically respected and, unless they can step out of their roles and speak from their own spiritual experience, they lack credibility.

Despite difficulties in recruitment, religious orders are increasingly cautious about whom they admit. They are more alert to the lonely, inadequate and immature — those who fear being alone and are simply looking for shelter. Postulants are no longer accepted straight from school. They are encouraged to go out and establish themselves among their peers, live independently, and train for useful jobs with good salaries. It is impressed on them that no community is a soft option. Along with the rigorous call to poverty, chastity and obedience, there is no longer the absolute certainty of a lifelong safe haven in a world where the very existence of religious houses is in jeopardy. There is a lot to give up and less in the way of compensatory reward than there used to be.

And yet there are still vocations, even though they trickle rather than come in streams. Candidates are few, but more sure of the difference between career and vocation. The latter is not about being a success or competing with others, or making money. Of course this does not mean that one acquires sainthood overnight and many monks and nuns do covet senior positions within the hierarchy; yet such roles can be a distraction, if not a downright nuisance, when the real call is to a life of prayer, to love and serve God, and to minister lovingly to other human beings.

Twenty-five religious communities in the United Kingdom were asked how the phenomena of age and longevity had affected their common life. Twenty of these were convents, four were monasteries, and there was also a unique community for women, whose members retire and move away at sixty. (This we have described in Chapter 4, in which we also discussed the attitudes to retirement outlined in a report from the Association of Senior Religious.) The communities that responded to our letters cover a wide geographical span from Sussex to Scotland. They vary considerably in size, but in all of them the proportion of elderly people is high. To quote some examples: of the women's communities, one in Oxfordshire is down to three members, all seventy-nine and over; in Sussex, eleven out of fourteen are sixty-plus (with five over eighty); a West Country order has a majority of over-seventies, with one nonagenarian; a Midlands order, of fourteen members, has two under fifty, three over ninety, and an average age of seventy-nine; a male community, also in the West Country, has twelve members with an age range of twenty-seven to eighty-six, five of whom are octogenarians.

Thus religious orders everywhere are having to reassess their aims and identities and all sorts of new models of community life are being explored. One direct response to the dearth of young vocations is a new Roman Catholic order, established in 1982 at Monks Kirby in Warwickshire. This has been founded with the special purpose of attending to the spiritual needs of older women, including the widowed, divorced and retired. Those who join in this experiment are warned that adjustment may be particularly hard at their age and they need to show that they can easily return to their previous lives if things do not work out. This means retaining sufficient resources to buy a home and, probably, a car. Those still following careers are discouraged from giving up their jobs unless they can easily go back to them. It has been found that many who come for the initial three months' trial are daunted by having to get on amicably with strangers. In some cases, they actually get ill, often with a sudden flare-up of previous ailments. But one sister has commented, 'Providence is arranging for us older ones, who have nothing to do, to take over.'

Founding a new order for the old does not help the existing communities to survive. All those who responded to our enquiries acknowledged the difficulty of continuing their work and prayer life, while at the same time caring for the more helpless among them. The Assistant General of one of the largest Anglican communities admitted that they had only recently begun planning realistically for the future:

> We have done our best to provide good ongoing care for the elderly infirm, increasing the provision of care on our infirmary wing and doing our best to provide some assistance for our aged members who were not yet on infirmary but needing some care. Otherwise we were coping in a reactive way, trying to maintain 'business as usual'. Now we are trying to get ahead, forecast probable numbers in the different age groups and look carefully at the proportions of older members to younger ones. This proportion is very heavily weighted on the side of the elderly. We want to plan as wisely and creatively as possible, regarding it as the situation within which we find God's will for us at the present time.

One 'problem' or 'challenge' is that monks and nuns actually live longer than the general average age. A disciplined life, hard but regular work, and a strict routine seem to be life-lengthening. Here are some comments from a monastery in the north of England:

> During the last seven years, five of our brothers have died. Four were well over eighty and the youngest seventy-six. If people survive the stressful forties and fifties, they can look forward to a ripe old age. . . . Religious never retire officially. They usually manage to hold down some job or other in community which makes them feel needed. In fact,

many hold down important jobs well into their seventies and eighties which they are quite competent of fulfilling.

It is interesting that the middle years are the most stressful. For the average person outside such a community, one gets the impression that retirement (especially for men) is the greatest trauma, and that those men who get through the sixties will be the ones most likely to live on and keep up with their female counterparts. Letters from convents reported quite a few nuns living to a hundred and beyond.

Longevity may have something to do with personal problems being borne communally. As individuals, there are undoubtedly fewer decisions to make within communities, and, without personal possessions and income, life is much simplified. Those in authority have as many worries as the rest of us in that they have responsibility for the welfare of all their members and, as already mentioned, an uncertain future to cater for. On the other hand, those at the top do not stay indefinitely. Reverend Mothers and their male equivalents are elected for a fixed term of office, after which, instead of a golden handshake followed by inactivity, they resume humble status and equality with all the rest, usually managing 'to hold down some job or other' for as long as they feel able. Seniority is transient. What needs to endure is vocation. If that remains steady, the elderly with 'some job or other' to do in community have less cause than their worldly contemporaries to feel diminished.

One rather diffident scholar taught Latin in a girls' school. She was so interesting to talk to that her pupils had no trouble in distracting her from Caesar's Gallic Wars. When they failed their exams, she was put in charge of the kitchens. The pupils felt guilty, but she did not herself seem to regard this move as a punishment for failure. She took a lively interest in the kitchens as she did in all the varied jobs she was given. The convent published a slim book of her poetry, in which she wrote of old age, of Time's 'ambiguous gifts' and in praise of insecurity:

> I ask clear eyes to see
> My poverty.
> I go unguarded through a foreign land . . .[1]

Another poem was about a 'Call Girl'. She was more in touch with the contemporary world than anyone, at a casual meeting, would guess.

Religious houses try not to segregate the generations and this seems to contribute to health and psychological well-being. One doctor who treated the brothers in a male community told their Superior that he found them more alert, physically and mentally, than men of comparable age whom he met on his daily rounds.

All communities aim to keep their older members within the physical surroundings of the Mother House till the end of their lives and many still have infirmaries where this can be done (though, increasingly, the really old may have to spend time in hospitals or nursing homes when there is a need for intensive care). The closing of one Mother House, with space and staff to attend to the illnesses of its male members, actually proved beneficial. Threatened with being sent off to a secular hospital, none of the brothers became chronically ill!

What has made for stability in the past, and perhaps also longevity, is that although specific jobs varied and came to an end, the routine of the daily office, and the companionship of familiar figures, were expected to remain unchanged. Individuals would be posted to branch houses, either in Britain or overseas, but they always returned to the Mother House, which remained in the same place. The trauma of moving house has not been the fate of individual religious, who, for all their wanderings, could be sure of a final 'coming home' before they died.

Such has been the tradition. Up till about fifty years ago, there were religious houses, both Roman Catholic and Anglican, which were endowed with enough wealth and man- (or woman-) power to found schools, hospitals, rescue homes and homes for the aged. We thought of these individuals as living behind closed walls, emerging only in pairs and restricted in how much they were allowed to socialize (even with close relatives). Forty years ago, a nun was not allowed to go to her sister's wedding reception. Now the doors are opening fast and we can look at each other more clearly. Our view of 'them' as mysteriously 'other' has been overturned.

So, to some extent, has their view of themselves as specially set apart.

Monks and nuns who entered their orders in the first decades of this century, bringing with them the social mores of a post-Victorian upbringing, have adapted well to the changing face of the present-day novitiate. Those joining today often come from broken homes and have a less settled background. They bring different expectations and more questioning attitudes to the religious life. The way these old and young have weathered the shocks of the generation gap, their ingenuity, imagination and willingness to take risks, is a refreshing example to us all.

The monolithic institutions of the past are being replaced by local, community-based units where the 'small is beautiful' philosophy prevails. It is not uncommon, in inner-city estates, to find, not a convent, but a modest house with only three or four occupants. Perhaps only one will be in full-time or part-time work. Another may be a pensioner, adding what she receives from the state to the common kitty. We do not always realize that no religious receives a salary from the Church unless actively engaged in parish work. Each community pays its way and bears the cost of caring for those who are too old to work. Some have looked ahead and bought into a pension scheme, thus insuring a source of income as their members reach old age. These small households are structured by the usual daily office and a simple life-style. As microcosms of their parent communities, they are oases in the urban wilderness and can give hospitality and affirmation to the local people, especially the old and lonely, with whom they can share a spirituality focused on 'being' rather than energetically 'doing'.

Ideally, in such communities we see patterns of small families within extended families, and no individual members becoming isolated as is often the case in the blood-related, but scattered, families of today's secular society. The old are not put into a special category. Their worth is taken for granted. When everyone's central job is prayer, the old are ahead in experience, and this applies even if some of them fall asleep on their knees. Prayer is recognized as a twofold occupation, with God taking over where humans fail. As one sister said:

> Certainly, growing old brings a greater compassion for the world, and so a greater incentive to intercession. However, like most things, prayer becomes more difficult. I can no longer concentrate for long. I can't remember what I've read. I can't stay in one position for so long . . . this doesn't worry me. . . . I know that my life is in God's hands. What I can't give him, he doesn't ask of me.

Care of the older sisters has always been part of each novice's expected routine. In accordance with the 'family model', one convent, recognizing the benefit of mixing the generations, developed a 'Granny System', whereby a young sister was 'attached' to a much older one and they 'worked on this relationship together in any way the pair found helpful'. This resulted in a sharing of feelings as well as practical problems. As one sister commented: 'Not only have there been the usual things — writing letters for a semi-blind sister — but, on a spiritual level, it has been most rewarding.'

Living cheek by jowl, even with one's own peer group, can be frustrating, irritating and claustrophobic. Perhaps patience between generations is learnt the hard way: having patience both with each other's idiosyncracies and with oneself.

The oldest brother in one small community runs the laundry and cooks supper, but has opted out of the normal communal life including meetings and the daily offices. For worship he takes himself to the parish church. He walks a mile or so a day, accompanied by his pet rabbit. His superiors do not try and change his ways.

One sister says of herself: 'Everyone expects that I shall go on doing such jobs as are within my failing powers, but they do not *demand* that I do them. I am able to work without the pressure that was often upon me when I was younger . . . I need to arrange my time according to how my body feels . . .'

But another commented: 'I am not a child or an imbecile because I can't hear or see as well as I did. I am often in a certain amount of pain and am nearly always very tired. I easily get irritable, and they appear to pay no attention to this . . .'

It may come as a surprise to some of us that these ageing monks and nuns seem to show more tolerance towards each other, and also to be more realistically in touch with their own feelings, than many of their worldly counterparts who are in touch with life's mixed blessings. One brother said: 'It is a blessing to a community to have an invalid within its ranks, just as a handicapped child can be a blessing.'

But however willingly the young look after the old, these once capable workers must find it a great hardship to give in and let go. Old age may be a time for them to take back some of the comforts that they learnt long ago to do without. Gratitude for treats and minor luxuries does not come easily. In fact, it may be one of the hardest lessons of all to recognize that, in there being 'a time for every purpose under the heaven', there is 'a time to get' as well as 'a time to lose' (Ecclesiastes 3.6).

The mixing of generations in the family atmosphere of a community seems to work as well, or better, than in other family groupings, but the practical problems remain. When nearly everyone is an OAP, how can there be a mixture? And, without this mixture, how can the communities survive?

Typical of the current situation is the Mother House of an Anglican community that concentrates on parish work. Out of nineteen sisters, eight are over eighty and only three or four are under sixty. There are also three novices. Those in their eighties are able to look after themselves, but cannot contribute to the general running of the house. Routines have to be simplified and include self-service meals. To spare the novices from having to cope with all the domestic chores, some secular helpers have to be employed and this, of course, proves expensive. If an older sister needs nursing, she is sent to a branch house that is still managing, with a handful of sisters, to run an old people's home. Before long, this will have to be handed over to the local authority social services. Communities everywhere are having to withdraw from the work their members were trained to do and concentrate on the more mundane tasks of house-keeping for themselves and demonstrating to the people living round them what is, perhaps somewhat vaguely, referred to as a 'Christian presence'. This 'presence' was certainly very real in one small household in Africa where all races were made unconditionally welcome. It can apply equally in our own big cities, when standing out against racism, ageism and all the other 'isms' of our society. We are here describing not so much a job of work as an attitude to one's fellow men, and this can be maintained despite poverty of resources.

In tackling the urgent problems of actual survival, communities have explored a number of options. One is to approach a housing association and apply for sheltered accommodation to take care of their ageing members; or, more drastically, to sell their own property and rebuild it near a sheltered housing complex. This would offer support and perhaps provide jobs for the more able among them, who could offer themselves as wardens or sub-wardens within the scheme. Other communities have sold their over-sized buildings and moved to small, more practical, houses. One comparatively large women's community has opened its doors to some of the elderly members of those much smaller communities who can no longer manage for themselves.

Nevertheless, despite all obstacles, it still seems to be true that elderly religious are likely to receive better care than many lay people. One of the big bonuses is that communities behave like families. There may be bickering, bitterness and stress, but there is also affection and companionship, whereas many old people living in the secular world have no surviving relatives and have outlived their friends. Most lay people, if they cannot manage alone, have to depend on public services. Religious still have community help, however stretched that may be. Lay people may have to leave home and go to unfamiliar places for treatment and care. Religious are less likely to move and, if they do, they may still be lucky enough to go no farther than another community with a recognizable life-style. Even for short-term hospital treatment, a familiar sister or brother will accompany them and certainly they will have visitors. Upheavals for lay people tend to be more generally upsetting, with a greater likelihood of painful rejection and neighbours 'not wanting to know'.

Young religious can be relieved of some of their anxiety for ageing parents. Communities take on a duty towards the families of their members, and sometimes invite the very old to live within or near the Mother House. They also give sons and daughters leave of absence to look after ailing parents for as long as necessary in their own homes. One sister was allowed, on her brother's death, to take care of his ageing dog. The dog lived happily with her in the convent until he died.

The young in communities are expected to work hard, and looking after the old adds to this work. How easily the non-workers could be regarded as a nuisance. But in a society where a person's value is not measured in terms of productivity, the opposite seems to be true. One sister commented:

> We believe that our aged sisters are a precious resource of wisdom and experience and of lives given to prayer. We believe in the validity of the religious life as a *life* lived rather than work *done*. In the mystery of God's plan, the life of a sister incapacitated by physical infirmity and senile dementia may be of greater value than that of our most gifted active sister.

Old age is seen as a 'time of deeper transformation, spiritual growth, gentling, stripping away of masks and defences . . .' It is also a mystery. Even senility is respected and sisters make a point of praying with people who can no longer join in. Nobody is written off as too demented for participation and, in a life of prayer, even the most uncommunicative often respond with a 'Gloria', an 'Our Father' or at least an 'Amen'. Living in community means being in touch one with another, and joining as fully as possible in communal worship. Much can be done these days with audio loop systems between chapels, meeting rooms and also the infirmary, so that no sister who is able to tune in need be left out. Wherever possible, sisters are wheeled to chapel for a celebration of the

Eucharist, rather than receiving the sacrament on their own. And, for the bedridden, a group can gather round during a ritualistic blessing, anointing or laying on of hands, giving a sacramental value to what is tangible and visible.

We have already indicated that 'second childhood' can be a positive rather than negative stage. The transition to childlikeness, as distinct from childishness, may be easier for those who have never indulged in sophisticated pursuits. The pleasures of religious on holiday are akin to children's treats: picnics in the country, tea (rather than cocktail) parties, Christmas trees, pet animals and, very often, the company of children. Even to the scholar, walks in the country, the sun, wind and the coming of spring never lose their novelty. This is reflected in the writing of the unassuming teacher/poet referred to earlier. She called her last poem 'Short Walks Only'. This is how it ends:

> Age brings a special pain,
> To see it all, and know
> That it can not be so.[2]

We do well to remember that monks and nuns are not necessarily saints and even if they were, saints are proverbially difficult to live with. We have stressed the need for tolerance, such as was shown to the old man going for walks with his rabbit. He, in his old age, felt the need to move some distance from human companions, and he is obviously not unique. Having a room — or cell — to oneself, silence at meals and periodic changes of work, might be seen as wise stratagems for easing the pressure of relationships in the closely knit family of a religious house.

The sensitivity of interrelating in small groups has shown how helpful counselling and group therapy can be to community members, with the result that many of them are being given the opportunity both to benefit from therapy themselves and, in many instances, to undertake professional training as counsellors or spiritual directors.

As the retreat movement becomes ever more popular (and oversized convents are ideal as retreat and conference centres), these counsellors find themselves sought after, respected and needed. Not only is the mysterious 'inside' of monasteries and convents being laid bare to the secular world, but its inmates are showing themselves not as recluses or eccentrics, but human beings with a breadth of understanding and flexibility not easily found outside.

One old lady, who had been accustomed all her life to convent retreats and had many friends in religious orders, was able to carry into the old people's home where she fetched up in her nineties much of that atmosphere in which she had always thrived. 'I'm living in community,' she said, and was surprised at how many (somewhat less old than herself) treated her as a confidante. 'Human beings are *so* interesting,' she would say. She got special delight from throwing a ball at a demented lady and having it thrown back to her. She admitted that community life was not all a bed of roses, but added, 'You must keep your sense of humour.'

It is to be hoped that by the time the 'young-old' religious become 'old-old', we may come more and more to recognize them as the archetypal wise old men and women of the future, who can teach us both to live fully and die well.

And yet, the best of them would make no such claim. From the Orthodox Church comes the story of a monk who was asked, 'What do you do there in the monastery?' 'We fall and get up, fall and get up, fall and get up again.'3

Finally, our advice to anyone in a position of pastoral care for the elderly is to *get inside* a religious house for a short or long stay and experience the welcome that he or she is almost certain to find there.

What can we learn from those whose lives are dedicated to respecting people of all ages with humility and love? Perhaps the message is really quite simple: no ageism, no generation gap. All are equal and none more equal than others.

Notes

1. Sister Cyrilla, CSMV, *One Foot in Eden*, St Mary's Press, Wantage.
2. ibid.
3. K. Ware, *The Orthodox Way*, 1979, quoted in E. de Waal, *Seeking God*, Collins 1984, p. 82.

Part II

──────

From Independence to Dependence

SEVEN

Whose Home?

═══════

Ah yet e'er I descend the grave
May I a small house and a large garden have?
And a few friends, and many books . . .
Abraham Cowley

When thou was young, thou girdest thyself, and
walkedst whither thou wouldest: but when thou
shalt be old, thou shalt stretch forth thy hands,
and another shall gird thee and carry thee
whither thou wouldest not.
John 21.18

The word 'home' conjures up for most of us not only the place where we sleep, eat, leave and to which we regularly return, but is also a metaphor for belonging, safety and rootedness. Whereas people die, places and things endure. As we become the 'older generation', we tend to give a greater value to our home and our possessions. Rooms where significant scenes have been enacted are more alive for us than unfamiliar places. In fantasy, it is as though the furniture remembers. We may put fresh paint over marks made by people we love and replace mattresses and broken springs, but the memories remain. We get used to our ghosts.

In 'young old age', when we retire and have time to spend on domesticity, we may find ourselves lavishing more care than ever before on our things. Perhaps we pick up books we never got round to reading, stick our scattered photographs into neatly labelled albums and, if we are gardeners, find ourselves planting shrubs or even trees that will outlive us.

When we are widowed, we cling to everything that we once

shared. It is hard to achieve a balance between living only with our memories and adjusting to new possibilities. The process takes time and we have to decide for ourselves whether or not to make a drastic move. Is the house too big and do we really want to spend all our time maintaining it? We may be urged to join clubs, attend classes, take up voluntary work. People may say: 'You need taking out of yourself' or 'It won't do you any good brooding over the past.' Won't it? It is for each individual, not for some well-meaning adviser, to decide how much and how soon we want to cut ourselves off from our former ways of living.

Being alone, perhaps for the first time, is a challenge. The capacity for solitude, without loneliness, begins in childhood and it has been suggested that the healthy child first learns to be alone in the presence of a reliable mother.[1] Once we have achieved self-sufficiency, it is unlikely to be entirely lost, however much we miss those who have left us. Our possessions will be reminders. One sixty-five-year-old, looking at all she had inherited, found it hard to accept that she now owned all the furniture and pictures that she had known all her life — possessions remembered in her grandparents' and parents' homes, together with items that she had inherited from her husband's family. She thought of it all as 'ours' rather than 'mine' and the continuing sense of a shared ownership enabled her to accept living alone almost as though she was still in the presence of her family.

Eventually the stage of 'old old age' will overtake us. However good we are at coping with solitude, our independence becomes threatened. Our children begin to worry about us and come up with suggestions of bungalows or flats. Of course we want to stay where we are for as long as we can and we will probably deny for some time the effort required to climb all those stairs, or that we have too big a garden and more rooms than we need. If there is to be a change, what we most resent is that someone else should make the decision for us. If our lives are to be rearranged, it is important that this should happen when *we* are ready for it and not before — perhaps even if we learn the hard way by having a fall. However worrying this may be for children and helpers, those who have reached their eighties often have a dare-devil feeling of 'nothing to lose' and are prepared to take a few risks.

Whether, and how, the really old can continue living at home depends on circumstances, particularly on who is available to help and how much it costs. Not long ago, an official report by the Government's Social Services Inspectorate criticized the standards of services that the community offers: 'There is urgent need for extended and flexible services, with emphasis on supervised meals, help with putting to bed and getting up, ensuring warmth and night sitting. Without increased input from statutory services and greater involvement in the community, the least able among us will continue to be neglected for long dark hours on end' (*Sunday Times*, 17 September 1989). Individual cases are quoted — such as that of a disabled woman who was left by her part-time care assistant behind closed curtains from after lunch till breakfast the following day. Also described was the plight of a daughter caring for her old mother who, with a shortage of incontinence pads, was considering how she might launder those she had for further use. Home care assistants tend to be thin on the ground and only able to give a few hours' service each day. Day centres are too few and the transport to get to them may not be reliable. 'Is there poverty in Britain?' is a question that has been raised of late. If we are looking for a marked inequality between 'haves' and 'have-nots', we would do well to study our population in the over-eighty age group. A considerable amount of public attention is given to deprived children, but much less to the deprived old. And, when we think of the carers, working with children will always be a rosier option.

Carers range from lodgers, neighbours and friends to paid professionals. If offspring live nearby, they usually (willingly or unwillingly) take on the responsibility, though often with varying feelings of guilt and misgiving. Much depends on the relationship: in some cases this may be so mutually destructive that offspring turn their backs on their elderly parents and leave the duty to outsiders.

One solution is the 'granny flat' in a son's or daughter's

house, but it may not be easy to create enough space for the older generation to keep some independence. Ideally there should be a separate bathroom and a kitchen where the old person (or couple) can cook different meals and choose when to eat them. But, after the transition from 'young old age' to 'old old age', the time will probably come when this particular freedom has to be given up and the old need feeding and looking after in the same way as the very young. Restriction on space inevitably means giving away cherished possessions and the children who are offering part of their home may not always realize the pain of their parents' sacrifice. It is often a question of both generations fighting for control. Whose home is it?

These generalizations are best illustrated with some true stories.

George and Mary, with their eighteen-year-old son Peter, lived on a smallholding and grew tomatoes, kept goats and collected rare birds. They had several dogs, numerous litters of puppies and lived in rural surroundings. Peter had started work nearby. They supplemented their income with a vegetable-round and Mary also did part-time work in a local restaurant, so they were not at home during the day. It was a pleasant but busy life, with some worries about making ends meet and few holidays. The rare occasions when they could leave the animals in Peter's care and get away together were important to them. George's mother, now in her eighties, had been widowed for some time. Her husband had been in the Navy so she was used to separations, and was in fact more shaken by the death of her identical twin. The twins had met daily and shared all their thoughts. Mum had never joined clubs or gone in for outside activities. A small cleaning job kept her going till retirement age, after which she gradually isolated herself and became depressed.

George and Mary lived some 15 miles away and had her to stay frequently. George was her only son and, in her eyes, he could do no wrong. She found Mary acceptable, but the relationship was never close. Peter, also an only son, got on well with her. Mary's own mother had died uncomplainingly of cancer long before she became old and dependent. George's mother made the most of every ache and suffered from her 'nerves'. She had nothing else to talk about. George and Mary worried about not living nearer to her and thought they had found a solution when a sheltered flat became vacant in their village. They took Mum to see it, but she refused to apply. Soon afterwards she began having 'funny turns' and had to be hospitalized.

It soon became obvious that she was no longer fit to live on her own so she went straight from hospital to stay with George and Mary for an unspecified time. George was sensitive about his mother's growing confusion, which Mary had been noticing for some time. He and Mary tried to get her interested in their garden and animals, but nothing seemed to enliven her. She found reading difficult, showed little interest in television, and took a dislike to Mary's dogs. Her easiest relationship was with Peter, though she frightened him late one night by getting in a panic while he was 'granny sitting'.

George had planned a trip abroad with a friend. Mary was happy to stay with the animals and her outside jobs, but did not feel she could attend to Mum full time. Thus they found her a place in a nursing home. A social worker visited and tactfully put it to Mum that she was being given a holiday. At first she was pleased, then felt uncertain. Nevertheless, George and Mary were determined to try out the nursing home. 'Perhaps she'll find someone there to moan with,' said Mary, 'she's only happy when she's miserable.'

When she returned from the nursing home, Mum picked up the post. It was her birthday, but everything was for George and Mary. She opened the letters, did not understand the writing, and tore them up.

Whose home was it?

*   *   *

Trouble with mothers-in-law seems only too frequent and is not always a joke. Mrs J, in her late eighties, had a son and daughter who were both married with children. Soon after her husband died, she sold her house and gave half the proceeds to her daughter. With the other half she bought a house for her son, which included a granny flat for herself. She managed her own life and needed little help, but her daughter-in-law seldom spoke to her and resented six-year-old Anna spending time with Granny. Mrs J was sad but discreet. When her daughter-in-law was expecting her second child, she asked her husband if they could live on their own. So Mrs J sold the house that she had bought and gave the young couple half the money. She was the one who did the moving, leaving her son and going to live with her daughter's family many miles away. Here she shared the family life. They had meals together. Her daughter and son-in-law, although busy, found time to sit and talk to her. She also saw a lot of their children. What she lost was the larger space she had originally planned for herself and the company of her other granddaughter, Anna, not to mention her own son, who must have been torn between conflicting loyalties.

*   *   *

Another example of mother-in-law trouble arose when Mrs K left her small village in Greece to live in Kent where her son had settled ten years before with an English wife. He had done well and was able to buy his mother a comfortable flat, five minutes' walk from his own home. He visited her two or three times a week and was kind, but he was always in a hurry. His wife looked in every second day with a cooked meal for Mrs K to re-heat. She also brought the household ironing so that the old lady could help them out and feel useful. However, Mrs K could only speak Greek and depended on her son's visits for conversation. There was little communication with her daughter-in-law.

When the couple went on holiday, they employed a non-Greek-speaking companion who worked hard at establishing some rapport. At first Mrs K was often in tears. But with gestures and a few words, the companion learnt some Greek cooking. She took Mrs K out in the car to shops and garden centres. After only three days, Mrs K forgot to cry. She would burst into laughter rather than tears, and sometimes she begged for a hug and a kiss. One night she even woke her companion in order to share her joy at the beauty of the full moon.

When her son came back two weeks later, his mother was transformed. While he and his wife stood motionless in surprise, she walked up to them confidently and hugged each in turn. She then began to chatter about *her* holiday. She laughed so much that it was difficult to catch all that she said, but they laughed heartily with her anyway.

Before the companion left, she saw the son's wife kiss her mother-in-law, talk to her and treat her as a fellow human being.

*   *   *

Miss M, a spinster of ninety, had been accustomed to an independent life and high-powered jobs. Right through her eighties she continued with all sorts of activities. Suddenly she had a stroke which badly impaired her speech. She knew clearly what she wanted to say, but could not find the words. 'I want that round thing' meant 'Open the window'.

Overnight her life changed. Her relatives, themselves quite old, thought the best solution was to put her in a home. They got her a place in a pleasant house where the staff were kind and they were sure she would be cared for. Her room was spacious and looked on the garden. But Miss M saw it differently: 'that exiguous, dark place' with 'bossy people'.

So she was taken back to her bungalow and looked after by a paid companion. In her own surroundings, she was appreciative and undemanding. She also loved her food. She appreciated being taken for drives, visiting old haunts, and showing her companion the familiar countryside. She felt freer in the open air. Even her strangled speech seemed loosened. On one of these drives, her companion said to her, 'You've been very active and suddenly you've had to stop. How do you feel about it?' She answered simply, 'Would it change things if I were bitter?' In the companion's words, 'Miss M sees things as they are. She is not resigned or trying to be courageous. She's just realistic.'

Old people usually cling to the hope of staying at home till they die. An eighteenth-century poet, Hannah More, writes of 'the sober comfort, all the peace which springs from the large aggregate of little things'. It is on these that 'the almost sacred joys of home depend'. By the time one reaches one's eighties or nineties, any upheaval is bound to be dreaded. It may have taken a long time to reach the position of 'head of the family', or even to feel 'mistress' or 'master' of one's own house. The decision to relinquish this responsibility may be the hardest of one's whole life, and this needs recognizing by others. Friends of the family, including those in a pastoral capacity, such as the priest, will find their sympathies torn between respecting the old person's wishes and the enormous burden that a son or daughter may be having to carry in trying to find the happiest solution for the whole family. Should the young be sacrificed for the old? And what a lot of guilt these anxious sons and daughters are bound to feel if they find themselves coming up with unwelcome suggestions about retirement homes or sheltered housing.

Ideally, the decision should be taken by the person who is actually having to make this important move. It may possibly be easier for those who are used to living alone and have no younger relatives to rely on (which also means having no one to blame for being 'put away'), in which case advice from disinterested outsiders is more likely to be heard for what it is, without emotional overtones. But whoever proffers this advice, be it relative, friend, social worker, doctor or priest, it should be done with maximum tact and openness. The approach needs to be: 'These are the advantages and disadvantages. If you feel the time has come for a change, the choice is yours.' One also needs to get rid of prejudices from the past. The present generation of old people was brought up with the remnants of an age-old dread of the workhouse, which, as a place for paupers and fallen women, had produced a folklore about institutional care as shaming — and, possibly, terrifying. And indeed, some hospitals and old people's homes have been built on workhouse sites, with some even using — though much adapted — some of the original buildings.

But institutions are not the only answer. What has come,

rather loosely, to be known as 'sheltered' or 'grouped' housing is a comparatively recent innovation. It includes a diversity of schemes, the first of which came into being some forty years ago, well after the immediate post-war concern with building restrictions and the pressing need to provide for overcrowded families. These experiments in special housing for older people were run by local authorities and evolved somewhat haphazardly in response to perceived problems. Some worked better than others, with a lot depending, as it still does, on the character of the warden in charge and how her role is defined. Should she be regarded as a housing manager, care assistant or residential nurse? The answer is seldom clear.

If, as successive governments have opined, the best place for old people is in their own homes, with help from domiciliary services, sheltered housing should be a way of fostering maximum independence. Some schemes provide a communal dining room, where at least one meal is eaten with other residents. Usually there are shared washing machines, and sometimes a common room with television. At best, these services are on offer, rather than being a necessary part of the package; thus the privacy of the individual should be respected at all times with no intrusion unless required.

One disadvantage is that neighbours are all of the same generation, so that new friendships between age groups are hard to come by. Thus one becomes isolated from the community as a whole, with resulting loneliness. Few of us want to live on the fringe of life, and many view with suspicion those deceptively paradisal retirement villages that have sprung up in America and are already being planned in Britain. A glossy brochure advertising 'a home away from home' sounds artificial and the emphasis on 'the young at heart' hints at a denial of the reality of ageing — accompanied as it is with photographs of gleaming swimming pools, dancing and sports facilities. Those confined to wheelchairs have fixed smiles on their faces, as if not to join in the fun would be letting the side down. One such community in South Africa is designed for the old and exclusively 'white' population.

Retirement flats — or sometimes small houses — range

from very plain one-roomed accommodation, that opens on to long, dismal corridors, to expensive private schemes with carpeted stairs, lifts and the atmosphere of a hotel. Both varieties can be equally lonely, depending on opportunities for human contact. Small clusters of flats and houses, near to shops, cafés and a church, would seem best suited to continuing an ordinary, and reasonably self-sufficient, life-style.

It is obviously preferable not to move too far away from one's home town, friends and family, and the isolation of, say, a delightful cottage nowhere near a bus route is hardly to be recommended. Some independent 'loners' resent the 'groups' of houses or flats designed to shelter them from harm and they may need to risk, if not actually experience, some unnerving accident in order to accept that some small part of their independence has to be surrendered.

Indeed, there are some who move into sheltered accommodation while denying it to their acquaintances. One grand old lady entertained friends in her new cottage, situated with its own small garden, in a tidy close near the middle of town. It was easy to guess that she had joined one of these 'groups'. Noticing the stair lift (which she did not yet have to use) and bell ropes dangling in all the rooms, a tactless guest asked, 'Do you have a nice warden?' There was a pause. 'Warden? Oh *her* — we don't see much of each other.'

A younger, but disabled, woman realized while still in her sixties that she needed to live among caring people. She took her time, while still fairly mobile, to look at what choices she had. When she found what she wanted, she sold her home and opted for a flat in a complex specially built for the retired and elderly and run as a commercial enterprise. She was able to buy on a long lease so that she would have something to sell if the time came to move on to a residential home. She appreciated living among neighbours, and yet being able to keep her privacy.

Some differences have, however, to be recognized. Neighbours are very much in evidence, as they are all retired and more likely to spend time at home than is usual in an ordinary town street or block of flats. Among them, there will probably be a few awkward characters — maybe even a paranoid lady who keeps her curtains drawn and thinks people are spying on her. At least she does not intrude. Others might come knocking on one's door with any excuse for a chat. Of course there is still loneliness and it is a bonus when one is able to make friends with somebody who shares the same interests. But it also needs to be emphasized that simply being over sixty — or even over eighty — and needing a bit of extra care, does not imply helplessness and inactivity. Most residents are busy and many still own cars and get out and about to varying degrees.

A lot depends on the character of the warden. In the case described above, she lives two streets away and has her own family, but is easily contacted by phone. If she is not able to come immediately, other family members oblige. The arrangement seems pleasantly informal, and her husband looks after the garden.

In most complexes there will also be a deputy or sub-warden. Apart from telephone contact, the bells in each room (including bathroom) connect with a firm who immediately answers the call, in a way that can be heard without having to pick up the phone. Often the bell ropes get pulled by mistake. When this happens, the residents are recommended to use the word 'mistake' or 'error' rather than 'accident' — which might imply a catastrophe! If the voice from outside is not answered, the warden is contacted immediately. She will also be the first to know if the resident *does* answer and explains her need. To most people, it is comforting to know that the bells are there, even if they are never used.

Where the local church is concerned, a private complex for the elderly is likely to get rather less attention — in the way of visiting — than one run by the local council, where the residents are seen to be poorer and more deserving of treats. It is worth considering that loneliness should not always be equated with poverty and that money does not cure all evils. A churchgoer once remarked that spiritual needs only receive attention when people are very young, very old, very poor, or very ill. The 'in-betweens' are supposed to give rather than receive. Living in a retirement flat, one is still 'in-between'.

Because one can still walk, shop and cook — perhaps even drive — and get oneself to church, one is generally assumed to be all right. It might be worth putting out more feelers to find out the truth or falsity of this assumption. 'In-betweens' are going through a transitional stage and that is not always comfortable.

An unusual example — at least in Britain — of sheltered accommodation for the elderly is St Mary's Hospital, Chichester. This is neither a hospital nor a hospice in the modern sense but continues the tradition of the almshouse, where hospitality used to be given to the homeless. Dating from the thirteenth century, St Mary's originally gave lodging to those who needed a bed for the night. Strangers or guests (the Latin word *hospes* covers both categories) were given straw to lie on, and had their feet washed after their overnight stay. By the sixteenth century, it had become a place of residence for five poor people, 'worn down by age and infirmity', who were looked after by a 'custos' or warden. As the tradition continued, one big dormitory gave way to eight flats on each side of a central hall. Some time later, chimney stacks were added for heating, and faggots were stored on the flat roofs of the rooms. Later there were coal bunkers, and today the whole place is centrally heated. The residents were expected to keep themselves and their rooms 'sweet and clean' and to attend prayers unless sick or employed in 'honest labour'. Those who failed to keep the rules risked expulsion. Even in these more relaxed times, attendance at daily prayers is part of the routine. The chaplain is a retired bishop and, for these privileged few, pastoral care obviously has a high priority. The 'custos', or matron, attends to practical needs. Certainly nothing about the place feels, in any negative sense, custodial. The matron had just been widowed when she took on the job. Far from becoming depressed in the company of the old and bereaved, it was they who gave her the strength to carry on.

There is a feeling of tranquillity and containment in this solid building which, from the outside, looks like a barn with its huge, sloping, tiled roof. Going inside is like entering a church, with a chancel at the east end, separated by a screen.

This is the chapel for daily prayers. The central hall is like a nave but can be used, on occasions, for communal activities. It is a surprise to be invited into the seemingly pokey cubicles at the side and find oneself, each time, in a modern flat of two rooms, plus kitchen and bathroom and all mod cons. Most surprising of all is that the noise of seven or eight television sets seems to cause no complaint, owing to the thickness of the walls.

Vacancies are advertised locally and occupants are chosen from an area of fifteen miles round the city. Thus it is rare to take outsiders and some of the residents will be already known to one another, have friends and relatives nearby and some lasting connection with Chichester. The present occupants do not seem particularly 'worn down' with either 'age' or 'infirmity'. The youngest is under sixty and the oldest is in her eighties. Some stay on into their nineties, if still able, according to the old rule, to take care of themselves and their rooms. The choice is carefully made. Poverty and some commitment to prayer and community life are still seen as important. Some suitable people have to be turned away because they have too much money. Those who are chosen have reason to feel privileged. Their lodging is free, apart from a small contribution to the heating. They are expected to get on with one another and contribute to the life of the community. Some are talented people, who write, sew, paint and help, as much as they can, with the spacious and beautiful garden. Apart from the flats in the main building, St Mary's also owns a few cottages with room for married couples. The matron and her assistant live near enough to be constantly on-call and can be bleeped when the need arises. Each flat, and also each cottage, is furnished by its occupant, and thus every one is different.

A hope for the future is that a hospital building can be added to the scheme, so that the very old, who cannot fend for themselves, may be kept within the fold of St Mary's until they die. As it is, no one wants to lose a member of this close family, and somehow or other the very old and infirm often manage to stay to the end — although this cannot of course be guaranteed without further resources.

There are always exceptions to rules. Miss A had no previous connections with Chichester. She originally hailed from Yorkshire, but came to St Mary's via Australia! 'I wasn't even Church of England,' she said. 'My only qualification was that I really *was* poor.'

She believes that she was led to St Mary's by a dream. It was a long journey. She was in Tasmania when she started having recurrent dreams of her childhood haunts. She felt that these were pointing her towards England. 'Dreams come true,' she said, 'but often you have to wait.' She booked herself a passage to England and stayed with a niece in Sussex. This was expected, by those who knew her, to be a short holiday and her relatives poured scorn on the idea of ever finding a retirement flat in England. But she was determined, and it was through the Citizens' Advice Bureau that she heard of a vacancy at St Mary's. Despite her lack of the necessary qualifications, she was accepted.

She confided, over tea and her own home-made scones, that she was still waiting for an important dream to reveal its meaning. She had dreamed of walking down a country lane with her niece and coming to a wall. Her niece turned back, but Miss A decided the wall was low enough to step over. On the other side was dazzling sunlight and a small, round garden. Down some steps was another garden, and further down still there was a view of a beautiful white city. 'That,' she thought, 'is where I want to go.' She woke without reaching the city, but was sure she would get there one day. 'In this life?' she was asked. She seemed to think so, but, as with her other dreams, she was prepared to wait. One might have said something about 'the heavenly Jerusalem', but it seemed best that she should find her own way, and her own words, to describe her ultimate home.

'Here,' said St Paul, 'have we no continuing city' (Hebrews 13.14). Miss A realized she was still on her way, but all through life we need our staging posts. At some, we feel settled and would like to stay. At others, we are restless and want to move on. Eventually, we may feel stuck, having reached, it seems, the end of the line, though even this is never certain.

Miss B, showing a visitor her one room in a residential home, announced, 'Everything I possess is here.' She was keen to show off the room's advantages. It was small but had a big window, letting in a lot of light. Light was important to her and she loved the south-west aspect even though she had nothing much to look at, only a very ordinary street. On her wall was a watercolour of the country cottage she had left behind, and its wide view of the Downs. She talked about her decision to move into this home. She gave up driving after a near accident, realizing that neither her eyesight nor her reactions were as good as they used to be. She liked to keep things tidy and became more and more worried at not being able to control her overgrown garden. In the end it was a relief, as well as a sadness, to give it all up. She had nothing but praise for this new home, which she described as 'not at all institutional'. There were only six residents and they were invited to committee meetings every week and given a chance to air their opinions. They were lucky in having a good cook and were given two main meals a day. They coped with breakfast and tea in their own rooms.

The cottage had been an important staging post. This was another. Living alone, she had found 'a part of myself I never knew I had'. Now she no longer lived alone and was adjusting to less physical space. But her inner life, one felt sure, was expanding.

In seaside towns along the south coast one sees rows and rows of residential homes for the elderly. Sometimes even their names speak of 'Eventide' or 'Autumn'. From the outside they tend to look the same, but one knows that not all are officially registered, and one also cannot help remembering a few horror stories from the media. Even *The Times* (9 July 1991) carried a headline recently that read: 'Old people in Care Homes are Strapped to their Chairs and Drugged'. We have already written on ageism and touched on age abuse. Abuse is news, but caring is not. In most homes there is certainly an attempt at care, but understaffing and patchy training, together with a lack of imagination, can all too easily depress and depersonalize. Small acts of carelessness cause unnecessary distress. A visitor to one home was served tea in a plastic mug which tasted of last night's tomato soup. She was bold enough to complain, but her mother put up with it every day. Many of these institutionalized old ladies must have been proud in the past of their fine china teacups.

It was refreshing to enter one unpretentious building, which showed no outward sign of being particularly special, and then to find oneself greeted by Mrs C: attractive, young and without a nurse's uniform. Whether she calls herself 'matron' is not a question one thinks about. It turns out that she is qualified both in nursing and social work and has experience of counselling. She has a staff of eighteen, which includes twelve care assistants. They have informal meetings every six weeks, with wine and cheese, at which they can discuss any problem, practical or emotional, that is felt to be urgent. Mrs C also does individual counselling. One feels that her staff are well cared for.

The nineteen residents are mostly in their eighties and nineties. They are not admitted if they are already senile or incontinent, but nor are they necessarily turned away if these symptoms develop. Once they have become part of the family, Mrs C hopes to keep them, but the very ill may have to end their days in a hospital with more trained staff.

Like most private homes, many of the residents are subsidized by the DSS and only have to pay what they can afford. Most of them are relatively active and go out — or get taken — on shopping and other expeditions. They have meetings, help make decisions about their menus, and join in quiz games and musical evenings. Some of them need help with baths and practical tasks, and some help each other.

A romance is going on between two octogenarians: a depressed woman who never used to talk and a hearty RAF extrovert. What began with his jolly, but kindly, banter, developed into a close relationship which is accepted by everyone. Their rooms are next to each other and there is much coming and going between them.

Mr and Mrs D share a large double room. It is Mrs D who needs residential care, but her husband would never have let her go into a home without him. After her two strokes, at two successive Christmases, he had been given little help in getting back to their upstairs flat on her discharge from hospital. And, when they got her there, it was impossible to get Mrs D down again. Her husband had to rely on very haphazard help before realizing he could no longer look after her himself. They then moved from one residential home to another, without accepting any as places where they could stay or feel properly accepted by the staff. At one port of call, they were put in an empty room without even a bed. No one had told them that they were expected to bring their own furniture. At another, they found themselves with people whom Mr D described as 'quite mad'. Looking round their present room, he said he had no complaints. His wife was wearing a dress of liberty silk, which she had made before her strokes. Her speech was slow and he was inclined to interrupt. It was a sunny day and he had been invited to go on a coach trip, but he would not leave her side. Mrs C and her staff kept telling him to relax, assuring him that they would look after her. But he could not bring himself to shed the burden of responsibility that he had carried for so long. Perhaps, as he settles down with people he can trust, he will learn to let go of his worries and find some peace of mind.

Mrs E was about to have her ninetieth birthday. There were plans to turn one of the regular social evenings into a celebratory party, but she was shy. She liked talking about her husband who was a scientist and had written books. She had done his indexing, but felt she had lived in his shadow. She cried a bit and wondered if she ought to think so much. When encouraged, she talked of some interests of her own: hockey and cricket. She had been athletic, not brainy. She enjoyed watching sport on television. She also liked to read — or thought she did. These days she kept falling asleep. One felt she was slowly sleeping her way out of life.

One regular visitor to this home is a silky collie dog. The owner brings him once a week and his job is to let himself be stroked and cuddled and to eat the biscuits handed out to him. One Alzheimer sufferer, confused and sometimes aggressive, always felt soothed when allowed to stroke him.

One was reminded of a friend's aunt who, also in a residential home, no longer recognized her niece. But when her dog was brought on a visit, each responded to the other as easily as they had always done. Humans are so unused to wordless communication that embarrassment and frustration can all too easily block their natural responses. There is a lot of talk these days about body language. There must be plenty we could learn from our pet animals and also from very young children.

In all these cases, a continuity of communication seems vitally important. Friends and relatives need to listen more than they need to talk, and when words fail be able to stay in touch — and that means literally touching — without embarrassment, as well as giving enough of their time just to be silently present.

Moving house is generally acknowledged as being one of life's big traumas. But the moves described in this chapter are surely the most difficult of all, and the movers need maximum help. When the parish priest 'loses' his ageing parishioner to a residential home in another parish, he may feel that this person's spiritual welfare should now be looked after by another incumbent. He hesitates to trespass on someone else's territory. But the old person, especially if he or she has been a regular churchgoer, is hardly likely to want to break all links with the past and, unless the move is to a distant part of the country, a few encouraging visits, especially soon after the move, are bound to be reassuring. Other links might be 'moving in' cards, the parish magazine and a continuing recognition of birthdays and Christmas greetings. A personal introduction by the former incumbent to the new one, even if this has to be done by letter, would also help in this difficult transition. It is these little things that make all the difference and can too easily be overlooked. The subject of pastoral visits to the old and housebound will be studied in Chapter 8.

How often does a parish priest get invited to bless a retirement flat or a small room in a residential home? If not asked, it is up to him to make the suggestion. This is an important change, needing its own 'rite of passage'. To bless a small institutional room will not alter its size or shape, but

its occupant may feel that it has been turned into a home —
perhaps even that it has been given a soul.

Whose home? Belonging to a place depends, ultimately, on
what you bring to it and what gets created by living there. A
person's inner space matters more than outward surroundings
and this can be re-created in many different households
throughout life — and also — as most Christians hope — far
beyond it.

Note

1. D. W. Winnicott, 'The Capacity to be Alone', in *The Maturational Process and the Facilitating Environment*, Hogarth 1976, p. 29.

EIGHT

Pastoral Visiting

Go in the peace of Christ.
The Dismissal, Holy Communion (ASB)

Before concentrating on the specific subject of visiting older
people, especially the housebound, it might be worth reflecting
on the 'calling' of the visitor and setting it in a biblical,
theological and also a historical context. Anyone called to be
a pastoral visitor is, above all, a representative of the local
Christian community and a living witness to Christ's love for
his people. The visit represents both Christ and his Church.
The visitor needs to be a person of prayer, discipline,
obedience and accountability. There is a discipline in not
'going it alone', but working as an authorized participant in
the care provided by the local Christian community. A visitor
without this sense of community can be a liability, because
he or she is in a position of trust and standing as a
representative of the Church to which that person belongs.

There was not the same distinction in New Testament
times between clergy and laity as developed in the history of
the early Church. The gap widened through the centuries, so
that lay people found themselves only on the receiving end of
preaching and pastoral work.

Various movements in all denominations have, in our own
century, led to some closing of this gap, though until quite
recently the 'ministry of the laity' has been more discussed
than practised.

Church of England Christians, particularly those in the
sixty-plus age group, may still be quite surprised to find
themselves visited and given pastoral care by anyone other

than parish priest or curate. Methodists, on the other hand, have always relied on lay stewards, as originally laid down by Wesley himself. During the First World War, the Church of England started a 'Life and Liberty' movement under Bishop Temple, which led to the formation of Parish Church Councils. Later, the stewardship schemes, which in the last twenty-five years have become an important feature of Anglican parish life, put lay men and women well on the map, by asking them not only for their money but to use their talents in a greater variety of ways than merely running bazaars and arranging the church flowers. Stewardship visitors were given special briefs to visit different households, reporting back to the clergy on what sort of commitment individual parishioners were prepared to make. They also, of course, picked up on poverty and need, as did members of 'Good Neighbours' schemes, which were also involving lay visitors.

Gradually, with more widespread development of training for Readers (formerly known as Lay Readers), both men and women have become increasingly professional in the pastoral field. In many parishes, suitable people are volunteering and being carefully selected by the parish priest and his team to take part in this important work of visiting. Many parishes are divided into geographical areas for which individual visitors become responsible. They learn to keep records and, ideally, they meet on a regular basis for group discussion and supervision. A good team might include general practitioners, health visitors, social workers and community psychiatric nurses, as well as less obvious professionals.

It is worth considering five aspects of the role of a pastoral visitor: (1) worshipper, (2) friend, (3) comforter, (4) healer and (5) reconciler.

(1) *The visitor as a person of prayer* Ideally, a visit, or round of visiting, should be started and completed in the context of daily prayer, whether at home or by going into a place of worship en route. A visitor shares in the self-emptying of the incarnate Christ in that he or she is immersed in life's ups and downs. The most sensitive

visitors may well be those to whom life has not been particularly kind. Their own personal difficulties are given meaning and purpose because of their prayerful commitment to Christ.

(2) *The visitor as friend*   The word 'friend' is misleading because friendship usually happens by chance and has a life-span of its own, which is not subject to the boundaries of either a professional or voluntary assignment. In the role of pastoral visitor, we need to give special attention to the terms of reference appropriate to our commitment.

(3) *The visitor as comforter*   The pastoral visitor is one who protects the visited. The word 'pastor' is a translation of the Greek word *poimen*, which comes from the root word meaning 'to protect'. The visitor, who may be seen as 'such a comfort', is the one who encourages and sustains. He is neither soppy nor a wimp, nor must he bully, boss or patronize. The comforter is the bearer of compassion and Christian charity. The greatest gift he or she can give is time and attention and taking the trouble to sit down, thereby avoiding that brusque in-and-out manner that is more like rejection than comfort.

(4) *The visitor as healer*   Listening attentively to what another person has to say is a privileged and humbling experience and probably the first lesson that any healer has to learn. One ought to allow old people a lot of time for voicing unresolved anxieties and hints of bitterness. To take an example: 'I have never spoken to her after what she said to me twenty years ago.' Who this 'her' is, whether in-law, neighbour or one-time friend, together with the reason for the alleged offence, is probably lost in the mists of time, yet the fact that pain persists gives hope, perhaps, of a shared prayer for healing and forgiveness, leading towards reconciliation.

(5) *The visitor as reconciler*   As the relationship between the visitor and the visited develops and trust is built up, possibilities may arise for reconciliation with self, others and God and, in some Christian traditions, this may lead to a priest or minister being specially invited to conduct, and take part in, the Sacrament of Reconciliation.

Christ prepared his disciples to go out two by two. What right have we to send out, or go ourselves, in his name if we are ill-prepared and ill-equipped? A period of preparation or induction, accompanied by prayerful reflection, must be an important part of a pastoral visitor's commitment.

When new visitors have been prepared and are thought (and feel themselves) to be ready, there should be a service of dedication, a 'rite' of Sending Out. (This has been called the 'Forth Bridge' launch.) Such commissioning may take place at the main Sunday service, preferably at the end. The visitors are blessed and told to 'Go forth in the peace of Christ'. Pentecost (Whitsunday) is a particularly appropriate day, both for sending out new visitors and renewing past commitments.

Sometimes groups of visitors arrange to meet for a monthly hour of prayer. This may take the form of a Eucharist, meditation, address and prayerful reflection, or simply a quiet time together in a room or chapel. Such meetings can become a vital part of pastoral visiting when this is seen as a ministry, rather than just another chore in a busy day.

We now have to ask ourselves whether there is any difference between visiting older people and any other age group. There should not be, and yet inevitably there is. Many people live on their own or are isolated in uncaring, possessive relationships, where their individuality counts for nothing. Often these people are growing old and their opportunities for change are getting fewer.

Pastoral visiting has been defined as 'people caring for other people, not giving a service but of being present, a presence'. The professional visitor represents the community or church family, providing a safety net for those in danger of isolation or neglect. He or she breaks down the barrier that separates the 'visited' from the outside world, and restores to that human being a sense of dignity, belonging and self-respect.

It is too often taken for granted that visiting is instinctive, requiring nothing more than a spare hour or so, plus good intentions. This is far from true. Visiting, as outlined above, requires a disciplined approach, a context, purpose and boundaries. Without such discipline, people should be deterred, or actively forbidden, to make visits, especially to the housebound and those too frail to show them the door. Casual, unfocused visiting leads to outstaying one's welcome and insensitively intruding on the privacy of another person who is not in a position to object.

This is particularly true for a considerable number of elderly people, who are pathetically grateful for any caller to their home. In spite of constant warnings from the police and old people's welfare agencies, bogus antique dealers, phoney officials, unscrupulous builders and odd job men manage to worm or charm their way in, then steal, overcharge or generally exploit elderly residents.

Making a visit to an older person should imply that the visitor respects that person and has an understanding of the background and upbringing that moulded his or her approach to life. A worthwhile visit needs as much thought, or perhaps even more, than an office interview or counselling session. Ironically, the jargon of visiting suggests a speedy in-and-out, casualness and condescension: 'popping in', 'dropping in', 'calling in' , 'a quick call'. The implication is that here is something to be got over with little fuss, no preparation and minimum personal inconvenience.

Even 'born' visitors should be able to learn and apply a technique.[1] Each visit needs to be carefully thought out in advance. What is its purpose? What is the most convenient time to visit? How long should you stay? What, if anything, do you take with you? It is essential to spell out the constraints imposed by the particular circumstances in which the visit is to be made. Because of fear of crime, many older people living on their own refuse to answer the door after dark. With the previously mentioned, partially heeded, warnings from the police, a distinct siege mentality can be induced. Reasoned discussion will not convince, nor will attempts to point out the statistical data that belies the notion that elderly people are the prime targets for violence and abuse. One pensioner commented, 'That's all very well, but if more of us were out in the evenings, the numbers of victims would increase.' How to counteract this anxiety is a real dilemma. It may reflect an internalized ageism, springing from a culture that tends to equate being old with being useless, so that elderly people only too easily see themselves as without value or even deserving punishment.

Dr Theodore Strouthides[2] is concerned about the poor expectations of the elderly, not only on the part of their friends and families, but by the elderly people themselves. Society expects old people to fail. Old age itself is looked on as a kind of failure or, as Prince Charles described it in a recent speech, 'Old age is the ante-room of life'. This problem can be aggravated by the attitude of some of the statutory organizations. The assumption is that elderly people want to have things done to them, that they are helpless recipients. The old Poor Law mentality seems to be still around, with the assumption that people become passive when they are dependent and feel they have to accept with grinning gratitude what is given to them. But there are also signs of a more positive approach to ageing, allowing more choice in the way people are treated and their ability to accept or refuse what is on offer.

Respecting people's choices should be all-important when it comes to calling on them in their own homes. There is always likely to be tension between desire for privacy and the need for human contact, and a lot of diplomacy is needed in bridging this gap. We know that, for some pensioners, days can go by with no caller at all. Isolation may lead to desperation and self-deprecation. But when the visitor actually calls, he or she will not necessarily be welcomed with open arms. There may be barriers of suspicion and hostility, which can only be penetrated through persistence and patience. Unfortunately many visitors do not persist and are not patient enough.

A lot of thought should be given to making a visit, especially for the first time. Why should the door be opened to a stranger? Visitors should be aware of the extreme importance of proving their identities. Those who are housebound and friendless are not necessarily fearful, but they may be proud. They deserve a letter by way of introduction, preferably followed by a phone call to arrange a mutually convenient

time. Punctuality is also important. Waiting a long time for
what has become an unfamiliar experience can cause a lot of
unnecessary anxiety. For the shy and resistant, it is advisable
at first to keep the visits brief but frequent. Friendship
cannot be forced and the ice may take a long time to break.
Being patient also means allowing ample time for each visit,
but also knowing when the person visited is getting tired and
has had as much of one's company as he or she can cope with
at one sitting. The old live at a slower pace. Their perception
of time changes. The years seem to accelerate, but fewer
activities are being crammed into each day. What may to the
visitor be no more than a quick duty — ticking off another
name on the list — is, to the person visited, an occasion.
Once identity is established and some of the initial resistance
begins to disappear, hospitality may be offered by the old
person: tea, coffee, biscuits, perhaps a home-made cake. It is
a rare opportunity for some solitary people to be able to offer
something in return for the time and attention of the caller.
The success of a visit may depend on how food is offered and
accepted.

H. E. Savage, as far back as 1901, wrote: 'In [parochial]
visiting it is essential to cultivate a sensitive courtesy and to
set an example of quiet self-control and unfailing regard for
the feelings of others.'[3]

However short or long the visit, the caller needs to find the
best place to sit. One may be visiting someone who is losing
sight or hearing. It is important therefore that one should be
seen — not as a silhouette, but as oneself with the light full
on one's face. Speaking slowly but distinctly is helpful too;
abstract and verbose statements are certainly to be avoided.
If what is said does not get through, the message must be
reworded. Shouting is strictly taboo.

Try listening to a record played at the wrong speed and you
may get some idea of how hard it is for the deaf to understand
what you say. Then try some simple devices to offset this
difficulty: short sentences of five words or less, pauses and
gestures, rephrasing rather than repetition, and looking at the
person you are speaking to. The voice of the visitor may be
high-pitched, in which case the need is to speak in a lower

tone, yet always with clarity and slightly louder than usual. If the person being visited wears a hearing aid, speech may be louder, but equally confusing because it is perception, not hearing, that causes the problem. Background noise is magnified as well as conversation. A letter board, a writing pad, hand signals, some basic words in sign language — all these have their uses. Hearing impairment can lead to extreme isolation.

For those whose sight is diminishing, some impairments occur gradually; others are more rapid. Spectacles fitted by an optician may be wrongly focused, for the whole experience of eye testing can be unnerving. When lenses are placed in front of the eyes in rapid succession, the difference between one lens and another is so subtle as to be confusing. If older people complain that their new lenses are no help, they may be quite correct in what they say and they need to be listened to. All sorts of different problems are caused by visual impairments. Sometimes objects are as blurred as a picture out of focus, or there may be dark areas resembling a torn photograph. We cannot always do anything to help the sufferer with this difficulty, but we can listen and use our imagination to understand how the problem must feel.

The first visit to a lonely person is a bridgehead, for it may lead to a special kind of rapport. Perhaps for the visitor it is just one of many encounters, but for the person being visited it may be remembered for years. The emotional needs of the elderly are the same as those of anyone else: to be listened to, approved of, accepted and esteemed.

One psychotherapist commented that, from the moment the phrase 'Good Morning' is uttered, a 'transference' takes place. Something of the sort can happen even in visiting: an emotional response that echoes similar responses in the past and may raise expectations of further friendly contact. It is vitally important that the visitor recognizes what is happening and keeps the friendship in an appropriate context, taking responsibility for emotions that he or she has aroused, allowing some dependency, but at the same time not becoming irreplaceable. If this should happen, the visitor ought to seek advice. The clergy are not usually trained to handle what is techically known as 'transference'. This phenomenon will be explained in Chapter 9.

One case comes to mind where an ageing spinster fell in love with her vicar and was heartbroken when he moved to another parish, especially as he was too embarrassed to answer her numerous letters. Life, for her, lost its meaning and she died soon after. It is doubtful whether that vicar, in his innocence (and ignorance), ever acknowledged any responsibility for what had happened.

There must often be an unconscious wish, on the part of all pastoral visitors, including clergy, to counterbalance their own feelings of loneliness and inadequacy. Visits to the needy may then become visits to satisfy their own needs. This is why visitors need supervisory help so that they may become more conscious of their feelings and motivation. Charles Forder describes visits 'to restore [their] humanity'.[4] Needy visitors may want to lean on friends, or on each other, and regular ports of call for reassuring drinks or 'comfort food' can be a boon, perhaps even a necessity.

It is worth concentrating more fully on what is likely to go on during a first visit. The caller is made welcome and offered a seat, or else asks if it is all right to sit down. One should always remember that one is a guest in someone else's home and behaviour and manners are therefore those we would expect of someone invited. Meanwhile, one will be assessing what the room gives away about its occupant. Cards, photographs, excessive central heating, pets, personal possessions — each item can be a way into conversation, whether one takes as a starting point a vase of fresh flowers or photos of likely grandchildren.

As they grow older, people tend to spend a lot of time thinking about the past and they are selective in what they remember. They often discuss times in their lives when they were younger and more active. While it is important for them to review these past experiences, they will probably be happier if they do not lose sight of the here and now. A balance between past and present can be encouraged through comparisons. An elderly woman may describe her experience in 'service', her pay and time off. This can be used as an opportunity to compare differences between then and now, with the advantages and disadvantages of both. Allowing and inviting memories of the past links it with the present and makes for continuity. Topics may range from housework to travel and public transport, medical treatment, church and school activities, farming prices, radio and television, family get-togethers, jobs and politics. Patience is needed. All conversations take a long time.

However, a good rapport may just happen, so that further visits are easily arranged. The golden rule to remember at all times is *respect for the person visited.* Christian names should never be used unless one is invited to do so. The older generation are still inclined to be more formal in sticking to Mr, Mrs or Miss. 'Ducks' and 'Dear' are likewise unwelcome and usually convey more condescension than affection. The same applies to touching. Physical contact is much written about these days, but does not come naturally to those brought up with different conventions. A hug could be seen as a great impertinence, whereas shaking hands is polite, and a good way of testing how much a person may value some form of touching.

If food and drink are offered on a first visit, the caller may wonder if a return gift is expected, such as flowers or a packet of biscuits. The best present is of course an authentic concern and, above all, turning up punctually at the time arranged. Any tangible gift might be a response to a special wish, perhaps something personal that reactivates an old interest; or it could be a birthday present. Anniversaries are difficult to celebrate alone, when those who would have remembered them have died or gone away.

But what of spiritual matters? There may be hesitation on both sides. The caller, especially if he is the parish priest, may feel something is expected of him — although not necessarily wanted. The person visited, out of a natural reticence, may feel that it is up to the caller to start the ball rolling.

In most residential areas, the Church has a lot of competition, much of which we may not want to emulate. Sometimes hardly a week goes by without a stream of callers from rival sects, bearing books and pamphlets. Immaculately dressed young men in pairs are often recognizable as Mormons. Others do not instantly divulge who they are, but ask if one is interested in the Bible. There is a recent trend to arrive in families, women with children in pushchairs, eager to give news of 'their' God or saying, 'My little boy has a message for you from Jesus.' Some of us might go so far as to regard the use of infants to push tracts as a form of child abuse. One gets to recognize the intent looks and unperturbable cheerfulness. At first sight, this larger-than-life bonhomie may be disarming, but once over the threshold the caller becomes an immovable object. For a vulnerable old person (or even a young one), this doorstep proselytizing is hard to refuse.

No wonder the pastoral visitor tends to recoil from this hard-sell technique and, in contrast, may find himself (or herself) speaking apologetically or somewhat dryly. Some schemes are purposely practical, such as arranging for visitors to go out in pairs: perhaps one of the clergy accompanied by a lay person or, more often, two lay people, bringing a leaflet about church activities. The first visit is brief, but with the offer of a follow-up — either a visit from themselves or from the clergy.

If the person to be visited is already on the church roll, or on the visiting list because of a previous contact, the visitor may like to bring a church newsletter, a service sheet or something like a cycle of prayers for people living locally. These aids may be an indirect (rather than hard-sell) way of introducing spiritual themes. Some visitors arm themselves with a prayer book, Bible, hymn book or volume of selected prayers, readings and brief thoughts. The theme of the readings for a Sunday can be a talking point, especially if the visited person has poor eye-sight. Some churches record sermons or whole services on tape for the benefit of housebound people. If tapes are to be played to a solitary person, it seems a good idea to invite a few others to join the service, thus introducing an atmosphere of fellowship.

Many of us are shy about informal praying with others. Perhaps both visitor and visited feel safer in church. But, once praying together in the home becomes a habit, it can be enormously appreciated, perhaps more than the visitor originally anticipated. In many cases, it can lead on, quite naturally, to an intimate sharing of faith and doubt and glimmerings of spiritual experience. But for some people this exchange of ideas may arise outside the context of prayer. It is wise to watch the gist of any conversation — be it about the state of the world or the family — to see if and when it might be appropriate to introduce a spiritual dimension.

Taking communion to people's homes is part of the sacramental ministry of the clergy. Increasingly, lay eucharistic ministers are being chosen to take the sacred elements of bread and wine to the housebound, either directly at the end of the main Sunday Eucharist, or on a weekday. This is quite a step forward in the pastoral ministry of lay people. At one time the priest would behave to these communicants in a purely formal manner, never making more conversation than was absolutely necessary before moving to the next house. A friend's elderly father was a regular communicant. On one occasion, after a ritualistic 'non-attendant conversation communion', it was noticeable how lonely the old man seemed to be. The reception of the sacrament and the previous short act of contrition and penitence, had greatly affected him. Before he could unburden himself and hear some reassuring words, the priest was off like a Jack-in-the box. Reverence for the 'holy mysteries' had made this priestly visitor blind to his communicant's human needs, and his all too short visit had about it the same kind of hastiness as that of a district nurse calling to give an injection, though probably with even less rapport.

If others — neighbours or church members — can be invited to make the whole occasion a shared experience, this small congregation would probably be able to stay on, to pray and meditate together, or perhaps drink coffee, should the priest have to hurry on to another house.

Most of us are not very good at handling conversations about death, and it is easy to change the subject when an older person talks about dying or a desire not to go on living. We need, as always, to listen attentively — paying heed not only to the words, but also to what remains unspoken. There may be some mention of helplessness and dependence, of being a burden and making no further contribution after a long, active life. The visitor may have to listen to a repetitious stream of regrets. To interrupt would be insensitive. The reiterated theme of being useless and not wanting to go on living may contain a hidden agenda of unresolved guilt and a wish to repent. Perhaps there is a real fear of hell. The four last things — death, judgement, heaven and hell — are rarely discussed now. Older people may have been brought up to hear countless sermons on these topics. Not to let them share their reflections is inconsiderate. We are aware these days of sects that give great emphasis to the devil and demonology and, with all the attendant publicity, some old people may be getting anxious. How important therefore that *we* should not show ourselves afraid to talk with them about whatever insights we have about death and a future life. And, once we are able to talk about death, why not be practical? It is not inappropriate to ask old people whether they have made their wills and left their affairs in order.

Whatever the theme of a visit, be it practical, psychological or spiritual, visitors should always be monitoring what goes on and keeping notes of how these relationships develop and whether the emotions aroused in a lonely person can be coped with and contained. To give an illustration of what can only too easily go wrong: a visitor from a local voluntary organization started making regular calls on an elderly couple, whose only son had been killed in a motorbike accident. The parents, previously frozen in their grief, began to show emotion. The visitor intensified the contact because it seemed so beneficial. The volunteer's supervisor became concerned that she was making many more visits than had been agreed. The situation was seen to be getting out of hand, so the supervisor arranged for her to be replaced. The effect was devastating, both on the volunteer and on the family who, having lost a son, were now deprived of the substitute daughter, found in the original volunteer. This typical story highlights the need for tightening up of supervision and for considerably more training in the art of visiting.

In some dioceses, groups of clergy have regular meetings with other professionals, such as social workers and psychotherapists, so that pastoral care can be looked at and given its own value, along with other services. It is sometimes seen as filling a gap between friendship and therapy. This can be a very wide gap, in much need of filling. Visiting, if sensitively undertaken, has a naturalness that tends to be lacking in more formalized counselling sessions. The visitor links the visited with the outside world, often bringing a 'breath of fresh air' into an airless home.

But sometimes visiting is not enough. The following chapter shows how the old, just as much as the young, can sometimes be helped to take a long, hard look at themselves in a different kind of professional setting.

Notes

1. C. Forder, *The Parish Priest at Work*, SPCK 1947.
2. T. Strouthides, *Agelines*, BBC Radio Sussex 1987.
3. H. E. Savage, *The Friendly Visitors' Handbook*, 1984, quoted in C. Forder, *The Parish Priest at Work*, p. 44.
4. ibid., p. 265.

NINE

Counselling and Psychotherapy

If you bring forth what is within you, what you bring forth will save you. If you do not bring forth what is within you, what you do not bring forth will destroy you.

Gospel of Thomas

The Spirit of Counsel and Ghostly Strength.
Book of Common Prayer (Confirmation Service)

Older people confirmed in the Anglican Church will have had certain mysterious gifts bestowed on them. Nowadays the language has been modified, with the word 'ghostly' changed to 'inward', but the gift of counsel has not been redefined. Paired with a special strength, inner rather than outer, spiritual rather than physical, more is implied than the dictionary definition of advice or direction. In counselling others, we need first to look at ourselves to discover not only sympathy, but also empathy, that quality of feeling that is both our own and shared — a suffering 'with', more than 'for', the person counselled.

The original meaning of the word 'therapy' is likewise not what we generally assume. The Greek verb that is its source has, as its first definition, 'to attend' or 'to serve'. If healing ensues, it will be as a result of listening, attending and understanding, in such a way as to enable that honest appraisal of self that we call insight. Both in sharing, and sometimes also in a clash of views, there may be movement towards change. We need, as individuals, to distinguish between what we share and how we differ. And, if we are not to be swamped by another person's anguish, we need rigorous

120

training in self-awareness, so that we can own what belongs to us and respect what belongs to the other, in all its similarity and difference.

In the last decade, counselling centres have become a feature of most towns in Britain, though many are struggling to maintain themselves on donations and the dedication of a few voluntary workers. A lot depends on being able to recruit enough professional help to become registered as charities, and also to gain recognition by larger bodies such as the Westminster Pastoral Foundation or the British Association of Counselling, with whom they may become affiliated. The aim is usually twofold. First, the centre offers a service to people in the community who cannot afford, or lack the opportunity, to seek out private psychotherapy; secondly, it provides a training for those without means, or the qualifications required, for elitist psychotherapy courses, almost all of which are centred in London.

In recruiting student counsellors, age is seldom a barrier. Whereas it is unusual to be considered for a psychotherapy training after the age of fifty, older, retired people may successfully become students in the more flexible setting of the counselling centre. In one provincial city, a current course comprises a group with an age range from early twenties to mid-sixties. Students spring from a wide variety of professional backgrounds: social workers, nurses, health visitors, teachers, doctors and, quite frequently, the clergy.

Whether training in counselling or psychotherapy, it is important to recognize the essential difference between the original vocation and the specialized skills needed for this quite separate job. A parish priest may find what he learns is helpful in understanding the inner lives of his parishioners, and perhaps this is all he intends to do with his training; but he would do well to realize that pastoral care, under the aegis of his priestly authority, while having of course its own validity, is a separate discipline from that of the counsellor. Most priest/counsellors and priest/therapists avoid wearing two hats in their parishes, but accept clients from further afield, with whom they work anonymously without their dog collars. They will refer their own parishioners, if possible, to a colleague working nearby. The same rule of practice should apply to the medical profession, especially to general practitioners.

To some clients, a shared Christian faith seems all-important, and it is certainly useful to have a common language that both sides can understand. But the counsellor is not a spiritual director. If he is a priest, there may be another time and place for giving his views and imparting wisdom. As counsellor, he keeps his beliefs to himself; in this context, they are not important. His sole task is to enable the other to make his own discoveries, however alien these may seem. Evangelism is not part of the counsellor's stock-in-trade. Much the same could be said to apply to the medically trained counsellor/therapist and his use of drugs, which most would agree are inappropriate as an adjunct to the 'talking cure'.

The word 'counselling' — as also the word 'psychotherapy' — covers what one might refer to as 'a multitude of sins'. Theories and practices abound and cannot be contained in one chapter. Psychodynamic therapy has not traditionally offered much to older people, and some of the new techniques of relaxation, meditation, self-help, as well as support, advice, or even tea and chat, may prove more suitable than a formal type of counselling. But many in their sixties, seventies or even eighties may benefit, just as much as their sons and daughters, from what is usually termed the 'psychodynamic' approach. By this, we mean exploring how unconscious, as well as conscious, motivation affects behaviour, making links between present anxieties and past experience and a thorough investigation of that which is popularly described as what 'makes people tick'. One of the main difficulties with older people is not that they are unable to work at this level, but that they are reluctant to try.

These are people who belong to a generation educated to suppress feelings. Tears, especially for men, have been seen as signs of weakness, and too much introspection regarded as self-indulgence. Sex was never openly discussed, especially between men and women, and certainly not among parents and children. Freud was still regarded with suspicion. At best, psychoanalysis was a joke, something practised by Americans. The English were proud of their 'stiff upper lips', and Christian teaching tended to encourage some of these attitudes. The emphasis was on loving one's neighbour, but 'as thy self' made little sense when that self had to be regarded as a 'miserable sinner' in whom there was 'no health'. We had all of us 'erred and strayed like lost sheep' and needed to be brought back to the fold of orderliness and conventionality.

Such was the enforcement of rules imposed from outside that we have come to expect a hardening of attitudes from the older generation and a resistance to new ideas, which is not, in fact, confirmed by experience. Those comparatively few researchers who have bothered to find out, have refuted this myth of rigidity in older people as 'a fallacy based on the metaphor that increasing stubbornness or fixed ideas in the aged is a precursor to rigor mortis'.[1]

Given the chance, the old have proved less stubbornly defensive and more flexible than many younger clients. Feeling old does not necessarily coincide with the number of years lived, and it is the young who are often rigid in stereotyping their elders as a different species from themselves. Just as we all carry within us both masculine and feminine tendencies, so do we retain many features of childhood. Children, likewise, often astonish us with an age-old wisdom. The course of life is more fluid than people tend to think. A worn-out body is obviously an obstacle to human happiness, but so is physical handicap at any age. Both biologically and mentally, we each of us grow old in our own — and not someone else's — time.

Freud dismissed the over-fifties as unsuitable for his kind of treatment. Women, he seemed to think, were finished at thirty: 'Her libido has taken up final positions . . . there are no paths for future development . . .'.[2] This quotation makes us gasp today, but we have to remember that during his formative years he was used to seeing women dying in childbirth. Not many outlived their husbands, as they are likely to do today. Despite our changing attitudes, Freud's legacy remains and there is often reluctance among therapists about taking on the old and retired. Some of this resistance is understandable. How can we explore what we have not experienced ourselves?

Counselling, psychotherapy and psychoanalysis are sometimes seen as a continuum, rather than three quite separate approaches. But, in taking this view, we need clear definitions of what we mean by each, since the terms are often used loosely to describe all sorts of different methods.

If we stay with the psychodynamic model, placing counselling at one end of this sequence and analysis at the other, we would probably agree that those qualities most needed in a counsellor are those we would hope to find in any good pastoral worker, especially when developed by further training. Most important are the ability to listen and *empathically* to share another person's inner world. Empathy is not quite the same as sympathy, in that it implies an ability to stand, as it were, in another's shoes, thereby perhaps being able to see even more of that person than he or she can see for himself or herself. It is then a question of how to use this empathic insight, either by a simple reflecting back (like the mother's mirroring of the child, mentioned earlier in the book) or by helping the client to deepen his or her feelings and share them more intimately. The experienced counsellor, through attending to repetitions, making connections and understanding what is being avoided, may start taking an analytic stance, and it is at this point that the frontier between psychodynamic counsellor and psychotherapist becomes blurred, as does also that between psychotherapist and psychoanalyst (and, to confuse matters even more, the Jungian analytical psychologist, usually referred to these days as a Jungian analyst). The distinction between analyst and therapist is often based on how many times a week and for how many years the process continues. Obviously, the more one meets another person and shares his or her intimate experience, the closer the relationship and the subsequent dependency that develops. Wherever we may find ourselves in this continuum, whether at the counselling or analytic end, the only frontiers we can draw with any clarity are those in our own experience which bar us from awareness of our potentialities and our limitations. We need to assess our readiness to give enough time, both to our own psyches and those of our clients, for penetrating further, deeper or more adventurously into the secrets of what makes us human. This is why all psychotherapists, and increasingly most counsellors, are expected to seek therapy for themselves.

It is often counsellors and students, rather than experienced psychotherapists, who are prepared to plunge enthusiastically into working with people much older than themselves; and this is through not knowing how the plight of their ageing clients is likely to affect their own fears about old age and death, let alone how the counsellor/client relationship may stir up unresolved problems with parents and grandparents. But all counsellors are required to be in supervision with someone more qualified than themselves, and are therefore likely to be warned off when necessary, or have brakes put on their enthusiasm for this highly charged exploration of unknown territory. It is probably wise in many cases to restrict the number of sessions and aim at a few well-defined goals. If the client is not helped, referral to an experienced psychotherapist is obviously advisable.

It is worth examining the real, or imagined, differences between working with a young age group and working with people much older than ourselves. One supervisor, approached by a colleague undertaking therapy with an octogenarian, said, without hesitation, 'treat her like everyone else'. One is tempted to agree. Being over eighty does not, in itself, alter the nature of a person's human problems. But, not wanting to be an 'ageist' may perhaps push us into ignoring certain realities, rather in the same way that our sensitivity about racism often leads to a sort of kid glove treatment when relating to people from ethnic minorities. Human unhappiness does not belong exclusively to one age group, and indeed the same patterns emerge in the old as in younger people. Presenting problems are the usual ones of failed relationship, non-achievement and loss, but with the poignancy of finality. Time and energy are not on the older person's side.

Pearl King, one of the few psychoanalysts to write about 'the pressures which seem to operate as sources of anxiety and concern during the second half of the life cycle and which lead some neurotic individuals to seek psychotherapeutic help, when they either have managed without it up to that time, or their neurosis has been inadequately or partially helped at a younger age',[3] lists five specific anxieties. These are: (1) fear of losing sexual potency, (2) the threat of being displaced or made redundant by younger people, (3) marital difficulties when children grow up and leave home, (4) anxiety about illness and dependence, and (5) the inevitability of death, as setting a limit both to achievement and enjoyment.

Whatever trigger initiates a plea for help, it is likely that all five of these concerns will be felt in some form or other.

An eighty-year-old widow talked openly about sex and seemed, with amusement, to envy a friend who still managed to have affairs at an advanced age. She herself clearly missed the intimacy of being married, of touching and being touched. She found it hard to let go of her only son and was disconcerted that he got divorced from his first wife, the mother of her grandchildren. Her mourning of this special loss, and the need to have it recognized, was her immediate reason for seeking therapy. She also needed affirmation of her various achievements and that the younger family should continue to share her interests, rather than crowd them out with preoccupations of their own. She was fiercely concerned for her independence yet longing to be looked after, terrified of senility (of which she showed no sign) and of being put in a 'home', but just as fearful about being alone when she died. So strongly did she want to control her destiny, that she hated to think of the world continuing to exist after her death.

It was important that her therapist should be considerably younger than she was herself and therefore not likely to die first. It was also important that she should not be too young to share memories — such as, for instance, the Second World War — so that she could identify to some extent with the anxieties of that time, and understand the old lady's guilt at having sent her child to America in 1940 while she stayed in England with her husband. The therapist expected to fill the place of the daughter she had never had, yet often found herself treated more like a mother. The seeming incongruity of such a relationship might bewilder an inexperienced counsellor, but in the timeless setting of the consulting room it came to seem quite natural. As in a dream, nothing is impossible. But dreams have to end, and endings are often hard to negotiate, which is why many practitioners do not advocate long-term or open-ended treatment.

On the other hand, why should the old, if they have time, money and inclination, not be given the same opportunity as their juniors to try and make sense of their being in the world? Many of them may want to grasp at a last chance, a time for repairing damage, not so much in the external world as in the timelessness of their own psyches, a letting go of resentments and the achievement of forgiveness, both of themselves and others.

For the therapist, it may be a long, hard slog. There is a quantity of material to be worked through, and this often has to be worked and reworked, for whereas an older person's memories of childhood are nearly always clear, an occasion as recent as the last therapy session may quickly become blurred. Both client and therapist need to repeat themselves, over and over again. The pace is slowed down and infinite patience is needed. The work cannot be hurried and it is probably a mistake to meet more frequently than once a week (though fortnightly will prove too tenuous), as the old person needs time to digest what is going on. There are also the twin hazards of regression and dependence, which the therapist will need to handle with all the skill at her command.

Long-term therapy is, by its nature, a risky undertaking and it is not only the old who become dependent on their therapists. The technical term 'transference' describes the illusory aspect of the intimate relationship that develops. It is illusory because of the anonymity of the therapist, who is sometimes referred to as a 'blank screen' for receiving the client's projections. Thus, both patterns of behaviour and expectations of particular responses will get 'transferred' from experiences with important — probably parental — figures in a person's past life. Over a period of time, and with a good deal of hard work, these illusory perceptions become recognized as not belonging to the present situation. Only when the projections can be withdrawn will the therapist come to be known as himself or herself — that is, as neither villain nor saviour, but fallible and human. Illusion turns into healthy disillusion and a gradual, probably painful, ability to let go of the transference in order to enjoy a relationship that is both realistic and equal. This pertains whether or not the two people concerned meet again in a different setting. Usually they do not, but this has less to do with rules of etiquette than the client's ability to stand alone or make new relationships.

It is often specially hard for members of the clergy to recognize their own need for therapy. It seems natural to turn to a confessor or spiritual director as the obvious mentor, but in fact this familiar figure may suggest a different approach. In this case there may be resistance to seeking help from a lay person, and perhaps especially if she turns out to be a woman. Indeed, in the older age group, those most in need of a 'breath of fresh air' from outside the Church are used to giving spiritual direction themselves. Both what they give and what they receive has proved sustaining in the past. Why should something else be necessary now?

In some cases, the familiar guidance may have been too comfortable. What was fresh and surprising to the newly ordained perhaps no longer has any effect when one 'knows all the answers', yet feels arid and in danger of losing that sense of purpose that was once so inspiring.

Uncomfortable questions may have to be faced. How much was that youthful vocation mixed, albeit unconsciously, with personal ambition? Did one pay lip-service to taking up a cross, which, only in middle age, became heavy? And, if one remained celibate, was sexuality denied or accepted as something eventually to be grown out of? Many clergy these days are daring to 'come out' and declare themselves homosexual; others have kept their yearnings secret and never acted them out. In an institutionalized world such as a college, there has often been solace at an adolescent level, but loneliness is more likely when a priest is on his own in a small parish, growing older with no intimate companion. A priest in therapy declared that he was a 'hollow man', echoing

Eliot's lines: 'Between the emotion/and the response/falls the shadow.'[4]

In the Jungian sense, the shadow is not sin, but an unaccepted, and therefore unconscious, potentiality that may well have been labelled 'sin' by the person who is busy disowning it, even when no one else passes judgement. The only 'sin' is to deny its existence or to project it on to someone else, and the only 'punishment' is the dissatisfaction that results. The therapist is not there to praise or to condemn, only to reveal.

An instance that comes to mind is a patient who used a therapy session to recount at some length how he had been let down and shamed by his son. He also reported a dream in which he had been imprisoned and tortured for someone else's crime. He often had dreams of that kind. His voice became a whine and he kept justifying himself and protesting his innocence, both in the dream and in the real life episode. Listening to him, his therapist found herself getting bored. She was surprised at her boredom and also at her inability to respond to him with any sympathetic feelings. She suggested that they explored together what he made her feel. He was sensitive and took what she said as condemnation. He likened therapy to the confessional and felt humiliated at having to confess. He could only see himself as a sinner or one whom others sinned against. This attitude was also explored, so that gradually he came to see the 'poor me' side of his personality as an avoidance of his 'sinful', aggressive shadow, which he projected on to anyone who seemed to hurt or let him down. How much safer, he always found it, to remain in the innocent victim role, seeking other people's pity and denying any anger, aggression or even pride in his own strength. He went away humbled (rather than humiliated) and less concerned with sin and condemnation.

The following night he dreamed that he was giving an exhibition of his paintings (he was not, in real life, an artist) and all his friends were buying them. His therapist chose the best and praised him for his creative power. He brought this dream to his next session, where he certainly felt she was affirming him. This patient was a man in his late sixties, who had always been an under-achiever, despite considerable talents that he hesitated to use. He longed now, in the latter part of his life, to find enough courage to take some risks and do more creative work without fear of being laughed at or put down. There was an urgency about his therapy as a time for filling gaps and also for accepting that he would also experience periods of emptiness, with no one there to assess or praise him.

Emptiness, for older people, is not just a state of mind but a reality. Friends and relatives have died, children have grown up and moved away. There are fewer people around with whom to share memories. However powerful the transference relationship, the therapist has also become, in a very real sense, an important friend. Ending therapy is seen as another bereavement. Sometimes feelings are so strong that all the therapist's good work may come to nothing if some support does not continue, even if this only amounts to sending occasional greetings for Christmas or birthday, tokens of remembrance when others seem to have forgotten, and also an assurance of survival among so many who have died.

Rigidity must give way to humanity. Nevertheless, there has to be an ending of the weekly sessions and the therapist needs to be rigorous in acknowledging a natural end of mutually useful work. More needs to be said about this, but first it might be worth exploring the twin hazard of regression.

This is another technical word. The ordinary dictionary definition is simply 'a return' or 'a backward movement'. In terms of human development, a healthy regression would be a going back in order to go forward, as distinct from being stuck at certain stages from which no movement is possible. Regression may be necessary in any therapy, but perhaps especially for the old, who want to tell the story of their lives, make sense of what has happened, and hang on to a continuity of being. And they need to get back to the feelings of their younger selves in order to experience this all-important continuity.

Some regressions have been termed 'malignant' in that the

new beginning, which is consciously desired, is unconsciously fought against. Infancy is a safer state than maturity, and even our elderly patients may refuse to 'grow up' and face a world that, as we have just seen, is likely to get progressively bleaker towards the end of life. To leave the warmth of the therapeutic chair or couch may seem like letting go of Mother's arms, but with *decreasing* rather than *increasing* energy, thus making it a huge effort to embark on new adventures.

Babies want to be gratified — that is, picked up, cuddled, comforted, fed and played with. Metaphorically, a therapist may be able to give a patient all those things, and most people are able to use the metaphor without demanding an actual holding of their adult bodies. Yet many of the old are literally 'out of touch' with other bodies. It is hard to make unbreakable rules (though many do) about never touching a patient. Sometimes a short squeeze of the hand, or a touch on the shoulder as a patient goes out into the cold at the end of a session, may give enough comfort so that no more is expected. Others can never have enough '. . . as soon as one of their primitive wishes or needs was satisfied, it was replaced by a new wish or craving, equally demanding and urgent. This in some cases led to the development of addiction-like states . . .'.[5] It is this addiction to therapy that can become a real danger with older people. Indeed, therapy may turn into a way of life, or the *only* life that is seen to have any value. Even seen as life within life, the whole nature of the enterprise is that it should be a medium for change; not, one hopes, a move backwards, but some sort of surge forwards, towards new and surprising experience.

To quote the psychoanalyst Balint again:

> The patient . . . remained silent, right from the start of the session, for more than thirty minutes; the analyst accepted it . . . waited without any attempt at interfering, in fact, he did not even feel uncomfortable or under pressure to do something. . . . The silence was eventually broken by the patient starting to sob. . . . He told the analyst that at long last he was able to reach himself; ever since childhood he had never been left alone, there had always been someone telling him what to do.[6]

This 'reaching himself' was because: 'nothing happened in the external world apart from the fact it remained quiet, left the patient in peace'.[7] On his own, or rather in the presence of someone he trusted, this individual found his new beginning. Another of Balint's patients needed to get up and turn a somersault in the middle of his room: an acting-out of an inner somersault, which brought the change she needed. These regressions are described as 'benign'. Addictive states are 'malignant' when they cannot be outgrown.

One elderly patient who had spent a large part of her adult life moving from one therapist to another, could only make an end by breaking away suddenly and starting again with someone else. She was typical of those who go the rounds, both of the alternative therapies and what the orthodox medical profession has on offer — anything to avoid being alone with themselves. Pearl King says that such people may 'develop a negative therapeutic reaction which is linked with the fantasy that by avoiding change or therapeutic improvement they will be out of time and therefore avoid ageing and death'.[8]

These words have been borne out by those who refuse help, and also by those who realize, however reluctantly, that they have been given all that they are able to receive.

Let us look now at a difficult ending.

The lady in question was eighty-seven and had been seeing her therapist once a week for seven years. When a date was settled for ending therapy — and this was purposely arranged in the summer rather than coinciding with the dark days at the end of the year — she agreed, but postponed thinking about it. Her therapist was keen to get her to agree to make a voluntary ending rather than having it imposed by outside circumstances. Good work had been done in coming to terms with past disappointments and accepting problems that could never be solved, but there had always been a turning away from facing death. During the last weeks together, efforts were made by both of them, but words petered out and always the subject was changed. Death, it seemed, would remain taboo.

It was only when the old lady came for the last time — at

first denying its finality — that she burst out with, 'Oh, I know I have to stop. As long as I've got you, I can postpone my old age. I'm putting you between me and death.' How exactly she echoed some further words by Pearl King: 'Patients may behave as if they had the same span of time before them that they had in their adolescence, leaving their analyst to carry the urgency of their situation and denying their actual position in their life cycle . . . and if they can manage not to be part of life, they will not die.'[9]

Facing death, for this old lady, was a further task that could only begin after her therapy had ended, and when she had to face being alone with herself. But one could say that the whole purpose of the therapy, right from the start, had been to help her face this ultimate aloneness. For a young person, the end result may be a readjustment to the cultural norm. A student returns to his studies, an executive to his desk. If we assess the value of therapy in terms of the individual's productivity, no wonder we shy away from treating pensioners, who contribute nothing very obvious to the enrichment of our society. And certainly no insurance scheme will help them with their fees. On the contrary: 'The real task and goal of analytical work with old people cannot be to readjust them to life, especially to an efficient and productive one, but is most certainly to help them gradually to detach themselves from life and to cover, without traumas, the archetypal path of life which is the path towards death.'[10]

We will be saying more about facing death in Chapter 11. Doctors, priests and relatives all have their roles, and not least the dying person, who may be fearful, resigned or pretend it is not happening. In therapy, the subject may never be mentioned as such, but is implicit in that one has to deal with what is 'there' and alive in the present moment. The past is talked about in order to give it a shape and hand it back, as it were, to God or to the unknown, completing a circular pattern of unity, separation and renewed unity, with death as the inevitable goal. Followers of Jung have gone so far as to speak of 'intention', not of the conscious will, but '*the* archetypal intention of life as a whole'.[11]

The past is remembered, talked about, forgotten and,

perhaps, relinquished. Some scars are reopened in the process, but talking and being listened to usually dilutes the pain, as each piece of life's pattern fits into something like an appointed place; and, once this is achieved, no further interpretation is necessary. Anxieties are about the future and its uncertainties. Dreams are of floods, long journeys and, sometimes, discoveries of new lands. This process, Jung's 'individuation', may begin in therapy, but needs to continue to the end of life. Death is part of that process.

Individuation — becoming more oneself — is essentially a spiritual journey, though not always recognized as such. It may, disconcertingly, have little to do with conformity. Whether religious precepts taught to us in early youth can still be accepted, or returned to, depends on the sincerity of our original teachers. In the case of parents, did we love and trust them enough to believe them? Jung, a Swiss pastor's son, sensed that his father's religion was lifeless and second-hand. He had to rely on his own experience of God for sustenance.

Sometimes, God, or the way to reach him, becomes real for the first time, but perhaps in unexpected ways. One of Jung's early followers, Frances Wickes, described a woman with lofty ideals who tended to despise anything earthy. In the course of a long analysis, she kept dreaming of a little black pig, who puzzled her by appearing in celestial company. She tried to ignore him, but he looked at her with a twinkle in his eye: 'as though he would say, "the piper of God likes me. You might too."'[12] Later she dreamed of climbing a ladder towards the sky. 'Looking down, she saw the little black pig rolling on his back contentedly, and she said to herself, "I will never be willing to climb to heaven without taking the little black pig along."'[13]

A middle-aged priest had a dream in which he was caught up in a computer. Waiting for the moment when he would be completely computerized, he said to himself, 'I'm not the centre of the world. God is objective.' Then he thought the opposite: that subjective experience was valid and that he could stand up to God. He woke declaring, 'The centre of the world for me is me.' He wondered if this was blasphemy, but felt liberated. Some time later, he gave himself a year to concentrate on himself and started therapy. This continued till just before his death, which was sudden and certainly not consciously intended. It was noticeable that he thought he wanted to talk about his retirement, but, without knowing that it would have been irrelevant, he never did. It was as though he were unconsciously guided by a force stronger than his limited ego or, one could say, he was in the hands of God.

Notes

1. A. Weisman, 'Psychoanalysis in Later Life', discussion from *Journal of Geriatric Psychiatry*, 1978. Quoted in R. Nemiroff and C. Colarusso, *The Race against Time*, Plenum Press, New York 1985.
2. S. Freud, 'On Femininity', in *New Introductory Lectures*, Pelican 1933, p. 169.
3. P. King, 'The Life Cycle as Indicated by the Nature of the Transference on the Psychoanalysis of the Middle-Aged and Elderly', *International Journal of Psychoanalysis*, vol. 61, 1980, pp. 153–60.
4. T. S. Eliot, 'The Hollow Men', in *Selected Poems*, Faber 1954.
5. M. Balint, *The Basic Fault*, Tavistock 1968, p. 138.
6. ibid., p. 142.
7. ibid., p. 143.
8. King, 'The Life Cycle as Indicated by the Nature of the Transference on the Psychoanalysis of the Middle-Aged and Elderly'.
9. ibid.
10. L. Zoja, 'Working against Dorian Gray: Analysis and the Old', *Journal of Analytical Psychology*, vol. 28, no. 1, 1983.
11. ibid.
12. F. Wickes, *The Inner World of Man*, Henry Holt, New York 1938, p. 189.
13. ibid.

TEN

Caring for the Carers

Honour thy father and thy mother: that thy days may
be long in the land which the Lord thy God giveth thee.
Exodus 20.12

It has always been human nature to care for the older
members of the family or clan and to expect that, when our
own turn comes to be old, our younger relatives or friends
will do the same for us. It is only during the last decade or so
that the term 'carer' has come into common use. When applied
to someone looking after a dependent relative or friend, that
person often responds in bewilderment, 'I'm not a carer. I
look after my elderly mother.'

Why this sudden concentration of interest on carers? In
May 1988 the Carers National Association was formed,
merging two existing voluntary organizations: the Association
of Carers and the National Council for Carers and their
Elderly Dependants. Between them, these two organizations
have had over thirty years' experience of working with, and
on behalf of, carers. According to government estimates,
there are 6 million carers in Great Britain, 1.4 million of
whom spend more than twenty hours a week caring.

The Carers National Association's definition of carers is:

> . . . people looking after relatives or friends who, because
> of disability, illness, or old age, cannot manage at home
> without help. . . . There is no typical carer; carers are
> ordinary people, husbands, wives, sons, daughters, parents,
> friends, who simply get on with what needs to be done
> when someone close to them, either gradually or suddenly,
> begins to need looking after.

136

Two years earlier, in 1986, the first ever parliamentary debate on the situation of carers was held. Among the surprising statistics given, was one that showed that there were more women caring for elderly or disabled relatives than caring for children aged under sixteen.

Two main factors need to be borne in mind when discussing this subject: the rapid increase in numbers of people aged over eighty-five, and current government policies for 'Care in the Community'.

According to population planning for the period between 1985 and 2025, it is predicted that over the next twenty-five years the numbers of very old people — that is, eighty-five-plus — will have nearly doubled, although there will not be a marked increase in the sixty-five-plus age group. Through frailty and illness, the long-living older group are likely to be in need of particular care and support. Fewer people will be around at the peak age for being carers — that is, between forty-five and sixty-four. More women in the twenty-five to fifty-four age group are doing paid work. Changing relationships as a result of divorce and remarriage, population mobility and the incidence of childlessness in the seventy-five-plus age group will further complicate the picture.

Added to this is the decrease in the number of hospital beds and places in local authority residential homes. More and more people will have to stay at home and become the responsibility of their families. On the whole, this seems to be the family preference, even though the strain can be enormous. As one carer blurted out at a meeting, 'You don't know what it's like till you've been there.'

At first the commitment may seem a privilege and pleasure, an opportunity to pay back in some way all a parent or spouse has given in the past, with evocative memories and many shared experiences.

Typical of this was an unmarried hospital ward sister, who took early retirement after thirty years' devoted service to her patients. The intention was to spend more time with her widowed mother than had ever before been possible. Plans were made for continental holidays together, day trips and leisurely meals at restaurants, without duty calls. Unfortunately, within a year, the mother had had a fall and was also showing signs of dementia. Now in her sixties, the daughter finds she has a greater commitment than she ever had at the hospital. She feels cheated as she sees what was to be a time of freedom and sharing turning into an unending routine of chores, with an incontinent and unresponding parent who has become a stranger to her and continually asks who she is.

People in their sixties and seventies, who themselves were once classed as elderly people, now have parents still alive. Sometimes it even happens that people in their eighties or nineties find they are full-time carers for sons or daughters in their fifties or sixties who have become totally reliant on them. This second-time-round assignment of full-time parental care is a disquieting phenomenon.

Awareness of the emotional toll of becoming a carer often takes a long time to sink in. A questionnaire was handed out at a conference in Hampshire for carers of Alzheimer sufferers. Eighteen questionnaires were filled in, which seems to be an average response. The first question posed was how long had the carers been aware that something was wrong and that the person being cared for required additional support. Answers were as varied as: 'Straight away when the wife had a funny turn in the night and the doctor phoned', to 'a year' or 'over three years'.

The second question, about what prompted them to seek help at this point, elicited such replies as, 'We were worried and did not understand what was going on, and did not know which way to turn for help', or, 'It was extremely frustrating that the GP dismissed our worries; we could not establish any credibility', or, 'Some close relatives did not want to know, and are still ignorant of what has been happening'.

A similar questionnaire, sent to ninety-eight known carers in the Brighton area, was returned by forty-four of them. The majority (that is, thirty of them) reported that they had to give some help at night, mostly taking their dependants to the lavatory or dealing with incontinence. The next most common activity was providing drinks. Several carers had to settle or pacify their dependants, often at intervals throughout the night. Six carers said that they had to get up several times during the night.

During the day, these carers had to provide a great deal of support. Five dependants were unable to feed themselves and another eighteen needed some help. Thirty-two dependants needed help to use the toilet and forty-one needed some, or total, help with dressing. Seventeen dependants could not do any lifting by themselves. Thirty carers also reported that they had to do extra washing, generally because of incontinence, and twelve had to provide special food.

As well as physical care, dependants have to be occupied and watched over. Twenty-four needed watching all the time for their own safety; seventeen dependants relied on their carers for all mental stimulation.

Nearly everyone had to receive help of some kind. Half had visits from community nurses, sixteen had day care, eleven had home helps, and another eleven had help from voluntary agencies. Only six received physiotherapy. None of them received Meals on Wheels.

When asked what help they would like to receive, mental stimulation and sitters were the most common replies, closely followed by home help, physiotherapy and day care. Four people wanted help with bathing their dependants.

The same carers were invited to make three wishes, and thirty-seven responded to this. Of these, fourteen wished for their dependant's health to be restored, nine wanted better domiciliary services, and eight wished for more free time. Six asked for more day care or short stays in residential care. Improved benefits and freedom from money worries were also important points. Other wishes included more rest, the chance to pursue other interests, more emergency back-up services, better pavements and public toilets, especially for wheelchair users, and also more appropriate housing. Only one carer expressed a wish to give up caring.

All this physically and emotionally demanding work is undertaken by one person with little support from other family members. They are expected to do on their own what, in hospitals and residential nursing homes, is the work of two or more people, who are able-bodied and often quite young.

As the House of Commons debate revealed, a large number of carers are themselves elderly, with ailments and disabilities of their own. Nearly seven in ten suffer physical injury as a result of their caring duties; nearly half are estimated as being at serious risk of mental illness. At any one time, about two-thirds of carers are in poor physical or mental health.

Accompanying this package of caring, there is likely to be emotional isolation and no place in an accepting community. As one carer in the Brighton survey almost screamed out: 'I feel like a hermit, walled in, and the walls are closing in and getting higher and higher. Soon, I believe, no one will know I'm here.' The more lonely a person becomes, the more difficult it is to do anything about it. How to retain old friends, or make contacts with possible new ones, becomes increasingly difficult. This kind of isolation feeds on itself.

A South Coast Care Attendant Scheme reported on how emotive are the dynamics of a family situation where a care attendant is introduced on a regular basis for an hour or so. The care attendant comes into the home to give the carer a break. This may mean sitting with the dependant, so that the carer can go shopping or meet a friend. Even in doing practical tasks, such as washing and toileting the dependant, difficulties arise in the relationship between care attendant and carer. The boundaries become confused. Where does respite care end and friendship begin? Some carers feel threatened by an outsider doing intimate tasks that have become their prerogative. Others welcome the care attendant as a long-lost friend, or the kind of confidante that they never remember having had till now. A survey among care attendants suggested the need for a personal counsellor to help disentangle the mixed messages received. Whenever a carer is isolated and emotional needs not catered for, a desperation for intimacy is understandable.

As regards a carer's personal counselling, especially in the case of a son or daughter — usually a daughter — caring for her mother, a note of warning needs sounding. There have been cases of daughters undertaking intensive personal analysis during this painful stage. As a result, a lot of past resentment and anger with parents gets stirred up, and inevitably the mother, now too old to cope with what looks like failed mothering, will be made to suffer, with the added danger of there being no time for reconciliation. It seems that what is more appropriate at this crucial time is supportive, rather than psychodynamic, counselling. Anything deeper should wait until after the mother's death.

Another aspect of the carer's isolation is deep anxiety about having to face the illness of the dependant all alone. Asking people into the house proves complicated if the person being cared for behaves oddly or needs constant attention. Getting out alone, or to join friends, involves complex arrangements. In the end, it seems easier not to bother.

One Brighton carer said: 'I would like just to go down to the pub for an hour, now and again, but I can't ask for a home help to do that.' (It is not often realized that one in four carers are men.)

Another complicating factor in the emotional overload of a carer is role reversal. Previously, the carer looked up to the parent for advice and guidance. If married, the partner probably did the practical things, such as driving the car, paying bills, keeping accounts, mending fuses, painting the house. These tasks now devolve on the partner/carer, who struggles with this different and unfamiliar role, without the accustomed companionship and mutuality.

Another loss is in the realm of sexual relations, as already discussed in Chapter 3: 'It can seem insensitive to think about your own sexuality when there are so many pressing worries, such as chronic illness and financial concerns. Nevertheless, people have a life-long need to be loved and touched. It deserves to be considered.'[1]

Here is a comment by a carer answering the Hampshire questionnaire on Alzheimer sufferers: 'After forty-eight years of marriage and only being with one woman, I do miss love and companionship, and have tended to turn my affections to a friend we have known for forty years. I feel guilty, so does she. So we have to cool it.'

Inevitably, a carer gets frustrated and angry. There is so much to contend with. Imprisoned with the dependant, avoided by friends, lumbered and left to get on with it by the family, overlooked as having any personal needs, how easy it is to snap. Exacerbating the external situation, what must be the carers' thoughts as they experience daunting, relentless, and seemingly endless, routines? Twenty-five per cent of all carers have been in that role for over ten years. They may recognize in themselves those very characteristics that they despise in the dependant. If children, they may find themselves paying off old scores, which have been simmering for years (hence the already-mentioned dangers, as well as advantages, of some sort of therapy to help them through this stage). Their own ageing, coloured by disappointed hopes and ambitions, gets in the way and they may start to view this new work with a repulsion, mirrored in the frailty and dilapidation of the dependant. 'God forgive me. I wish we were both dead,' said one Brighton carer.

If there is a religious outlook on life, God will receive a concentration of anger for allowing such a situation to arise. 'I get so I don't believe in God any more — but you have to — there's nothing else.' Terrible guilt can ensue from being angry with God. Does this mean complete lack of faith? Such questioning can undermine the carers, depriving them of the strength and reassurance that faith could offer just at the time when it is needed.

C. S. Lewis, in *A Grief Observed*, wrote: 'Not that I am (I think) in much danger of ceasing to believe in God. The real danger is of coming to believe such dreadful things about him. The conclusion I dread is not, "So there's no God at all" but, "So this is what God is really like". Deceive yourself no longer.'[2]

Unless practical and sensitive support is forthcoming, two things may happen: violence towards the dependant or the carer's mental breakdown.

The symptoms of carer burn-out include a perpetual feeling of exhaustion with accompanying sleeplessness. There may also be psychosomatic manifestations such as headaches, stomach disorders, skin complaints, general aches and pains, shortness of breath and irritability. All carers should receive a regular check-up: a visit, on a regular basis, from a health visitor or district nurse, practical help from a home-help, care attendant or sitter. They need respite-care and more than adequate financial remuneration. They are saving the state over £24 billion a year.

A pamphlet on the abuse of elderly people points out that: 'They (carers) are people with no specific training in caring or nursing, yet they have to perform the duties of a nurse 24 hours a day, week in week out, often single-handed. They are also emotionally involved which adds to the pressure. Most carers are naturally compassionate people. It is the constant pressure on them that may make frustration and anger overspill into violence.'[3]

Until recently, except in fiction, it has not occurred to most people that frail and vulnerable elderly people may need protection from the very people who would be expected to handle them with kindness and consideration — that is, their families and friends. The abuse of elderly people is too often concealed behind closed doors. Other members of the family, friends and professional workers are hesitant to invade family privacy. It is not until the victim goes into hospital that indications of maltreatment come to light — abrasions and lacerations, fearfulness, depression and a passivity that comes from not wanting to admit what has happened — either because of family pride or a fear of the consequences.

From British and North American writing on the subject, we get descriptions of typical victims of age abuse: those who are over the age of seventy-five, who are female, widowed or single and are therefore without status; those who have progressive physical or mental impairment, who are physically heavy to lift, immobile, incontinent, psychologically fearful and anxious, friendless and just as lonely as their carers. The setting of the abuse is the old person's own home, or that of an adult child; there may be other people in the household.

The factor of divided loyalties can easily be overlooked. Priorities have to be decided. One Hampshire carer commented: 'As a carer, I have an unhappy split personality. The sister I care for has Alzheimer's disease, and my other sister, whose younger daughter is a widow [stable schizophrenic], has a five-and-a-half-year-old boy. The child is the most important member of the family, we feel. My sister has to take second place to him, unfortunately.'

Abuse of elderly people may reflect a poor impulse control on the part of the carer, or unreasonable expectations of the capabilities of the dependant by the carer. Yet the mental or physical impairment of the dependant may bring its own problems. Carers, who have, on previous occasions been battered, bitten or bruised, have a second sense about when to keep at a safe distance in a room.

A strategy needs to be devised to prevent the carer from being completely demoralized.

Ideally, when it is likely that a member of the household may become dependent in a way never realized before, a family conference should be convened with everyone present, including the one to be cared for. This could be facilitated by an outsider, a friend, clergyman or professional worker, skilled in family therapy. Everyone is expected to be there; everyone has an uninterrupted say. A list could then be drawn up of priorities, problems anticipated and shared tasks. Who is to become the principal carer and on what basis can this heavy commitment be shared? How will the change of role affect decision-making on practical and financial matters? How far is it possible for the newly dependent centre of the discussions to get a full say on the reallocation of roles and responsibilities? This may mean opening up such contentious subjects as matters of inheritance and provisions in a will, or of giving power of attorney to another family member. And what effect will all this have on the younger members of the family? How will they react, for example, to a grandparent becoming senile and unresponsive to them individually? Children, fortunately, are usually excellent observers of adult behaviour. Their perceptiveness leads them to have a good idea of what is going on, even if they are deliberately excluded. Their resilience and openness helps them to understand that dementia is not catching.

In one family, the father used dried beans to illustrate his own father's illness (Alzheimer's disease). He explained that this illness made Grandpa behave in a very strange way. Like having a broken leg, little bits of Grandpa's brain had become irretrievably shattered, and as a result Grandpa often couldn't remember what he had just been told. The father continued to explain that another little piece, broken into fragments, made Grandpa get very angry, while yet another represented the loving Grandpa that was still left.

Teenagers may have ambivalent feelings about confused older people. They may be goaded into mocking them, but they can also be extraordinarily responsible, altruistic and compassionate. In one case, a woman in her seventies gave hospitality and sanctuary to her last living sister, who was developing Alzheimer's disease and would otherwise have had to be taken into residential care. As she settled in, the old lady displayed bizarre perceptions of the household. The two unmarried daughters, both in their forties, were resented. They were constantly asked who they were, and also what had happened to the two little girls who used to be part of the family (meaning themselves when younger). On some nights, their aunt would walk around the house, carrying off articles of clothing from the sleeping occupants of the other bedrooms. The two adopted sons, in their late teens, often pyjama-clad because they had nothing else to wear, were able with good humour to confront their strangely attired aunt on the stairs!

Lest the picture be entirely gloomy, there can be some compensations for the carer. It is interesting that, in the Brighton survey, only one respondent wanted to give up caring. Carers show a deep commitment to their dependants, even at the expense of their own jobs, health and freedom. Some find a new kind of faith in themselves and a confidence in handling commitments denied to them before. They discover that they can cope, albeit at first with misgiving, and are not out of their depth — or as inept as they had been led to believe. This, in itself, brings great satisfaction.

With very confused childlike dependants, a renewed delight has been discovered in sharing small things: a photograph, a song, flowers, playing with a toy or pet, a drive to the shops, a sunset. Despite the dependant's failing powers of concentration, these moments can be gifts, occasions for great intimacy.

A ten-point plan for carers has been drawn up, endorsed by a number of voluntary organizations.

Carers need:

(1) Recognition of their contribution and of their own needs as individuals in their own right.

(2) Services tailored to their individual circumstances, needs and views, via discussions at the time that help is being planned.

(3) Services that reflect an awareness of differing racial, cultural and religious backgrounds and values, which are equally accessible to carers of every race and ethnic origin.

(4) Opportunities for a break, both for short spells (an afternoon) and for longer periods (nine weeks or more) to relax and have time for themselves.

(5) Practical help to lighten the tasks of caring, including domestic help, home adaptations, incontinence services and help with transport.

(6) Someone to talk to about their own emotional needs, at the outset of caring, while they are caring and when the caring task is over.

(7) Information about available benefits and services, as well as how to cope with the particular condition of the person cared for.

(8) An income that covers the cost of caring and that does not preclude carers taking employment, or sharing care with other people.

(9) Opportunities to explore alternatives to family care, both for the present and the long-term future.

(10) Services designed through consultation with carers, at all levels of policy planning.[4]

Caring for close relatives is bound to bring pain. There is such a longing for the capable, younger person one used to know and look up to, and by whom one was probably nurtured, taught and supported. Too much personal mourning is involved to remain dispassionate. One expects, perhaps, in the more formal setting of residential home, hospital, hospice, or even when permanent or temporary housekeepers and nurses are operating in people's own homes, that carers will just get on with their jobs without undue emotion. But these carers also have their needs and these are not always catered for. One agency that sends nurses/housekeepers to families who can afford to pay for them, believes in restricting the length of time spent by any one of these carers to a few weeks. In many cases, only constant change makes the relationship of carer and dependant tolerable. Many people who take on this work are lonely and homeless. They have a need to be needed by their employers, yet they are often treated like servants or criticized for altering routines or cooking the wrong food. All too often, the carer feels exploited; her agreed two hours' free time in the afternoon is seldom respected and her nights disturbed by the whim of her employer. Often she is alone with the dependant and has no one to turn to. There have been some cases of sexual abuse and violence by elderly men. It can also happen that the employer becomes, in the lonely carer's imagination, a replacement for a lost parent, and is expected to behave accordingly. This in itself may constitute a reason for moving on, after a short time, to a new household. In fact, this may be the only way out of a difficult situation. However, constant change is bound to be unsettling, both for carer and dependant, and one is reminded of those children who have had to put up with an endless string of nannies or au pairs, rather than continuing nurture from their mothers.

All sorts of improvements are needed in giving consideration to carers, be they relatives or professionals. One often hears of young nurses facing death for the very first time — sometimes experiencing two or three deaths in their first week of hospital training — and how seldom this trauma gets properly acknowledged or anticipated, perhaps least of all by the young nurse herself.

We have mentioned one residential home run by a trained nurse/social worker/counsellor, who sees to it that all staff meet in regular groups and often for individual counselling as well. One fears that this may be the exception rather than the norm.

In hospices, the staff make real attempts to care for one another. When Cicely Saunders founded St Christopher's in south London, she managed to get across the idea of living in a community and that patients and staff learn from one another: 'So it is a place where life begins as well as ends, where people are by turns the teachers and the taught, the carers and the cared for, the workers and those who can no longer work, the sick and the healthy.'[5]

Another quote from her biography shows, as we have tried to do in this chapter, the importance of including the whole family, and indeed the surrounding community as well, in the care of its dependent member: 'I have a very good memory of helping friends to care for their father who was dying . . . on a farm in the country. I remember that strong community, the family, the family doctor, the life of the farm and the interest of the village. The whole thing was a pattern and everyone had a place in the pattern.'[6]

Notes

1. Alzheimer's Disease Society 1984.
2. C. S. Lewis, *A Grief Observed*, Faber 1961, p. 9.
3. S. Tomlin, *Abuse of Elderly People*, British Geriatric Society 1989, p. 5.
4. *The Ten Point Plan for Carers*, Kings Fund Publication.
5. S. Du Boulay, *Cicely Saunders, Foundation of the Modern Hospice Movement*, Hodder & Stoughton 1984.
6. ibid.

ELEVEN

The Last Lap

$$\dots \text{Last scene of all,}$$

... Last scene of all,
That ends this strange eventful history,
Is second childishness, and mere oblivion,
Sans teeth, sans eyes, sans taste, sans everything.
                    William Shakespeare

Sans everything? Nowadays we have false teeth, strong glasses and cataract operations. Shakespeare does not mention ears, but hearing aids are improving rapidly. As for taste, old people often enjoy their food and wine as much as the young. 'Oblivion' is not something to be measured from outside. With failing memory, communication with the younger world deteriorates, but, in this last stage of life, some stripping off of the known and familiar may be a necessary part of life's pilgrimage, a transition from one way of being to another. It is a mistake to assume that the generally accepted conventions of the things we should be doing, and when we should be doing them, must rigidly, and always, be the norm for every human being at every age. Being eccentric, in its strict dictionary definition, means not having the same centre as another circle. We can only judge someone to be 'off course' if a single circle predominates.

Old age, as we keep affirming, is not a disease, but some aspects of the ageing process are irreversible. An old person who is so disoriented and forgetful that he is likely to neglect or harm himself, must of course be cared for. This care should be given with the same love and respect as is given to a helpless infant, who, simply because of his utter dependence, needs to be treated as omnipotent. And, when it comes to respect, surely more is due to one who has already proved him (or her) self by contributing to the richness of the world, than one in whom we can only, as yet, see potential.

Old age is bound to bring diminishment of some sort, but it is not true that the very old necessarily become demented. Alzheimer's disease, much talked of these days, often makes its appearance as early as the fifties or sixties, whereas many in their nineties are clearly in touch with people and surroundings and retain their faculties to the end. It has been estimated that 80 per cent of all eighty-five-year-olds do *not* suffer from dementia.

Dementia, viewed medically, assumes that when so many aspects of the personality — behavioural, affective and cognitive — are affected beyond repair, what follows 'is not simply the loss of some particular function, but is in essence the loss of the person'.[1] Psychoanalysts such as Guntrip (of the Freudian Object Relations School) are quoted to confirm that 'self' (meaning here not the Jungian definition of self, but what in this book we have been calling the 'ego') depends on

> the intactness of memory, the ability to continue to interpret the present within the structure of personal experience in the past, and the ability to continue to extend this continuity to one's future intentions. The confusion that surrounds the dementing person is a confusion over reference points, both current and historical, which dislocates actions, misperceives experience and loses the thread that gives meaning and intentionality to behaviour, which taken globally, reflects a fundamental loss of relatedness to both the physical and social environment.[2]

All this is true as regards the ego, which to many Freudians is synonymous with self. In Jungian terminology, the ego is confined to what we have already described as that restricted aspect of self with which we relate to practical data in the outside world. This is sometimes called the executive part of the personality which, according to the passage just quoted, would be lost in the dementing person.

In Chapter 2, we concentrated on 'self-experience', rather than attempting any watertight definition of what the 'self' or 'Self' actually is. When, to all outward appearances, we are confronted with 'sans everything', it is not for us to judge that a person's selfhood has finally disappeared. What we contemplate is a mystery. 'All nature grows in the dark and it is God's providence which ordains who it is who needs that darkness of mind and sense in which the spirit can find its final consummation. We do not know at what perfection they are inwardly gazing, who endure this strange state of senile decay.'[3]

Despite the many problems confronting carers, we must all of us learn humility in the face of this 'strange state' and stop presuming to know what is going on.

Sometimes it is not that hard to enter into an old person's timeless world. One old lady, a few days before she died, asked, 'Where's John?' There was no point in sticking to the facts and repeating to her that John, her husband, had been dead for twenty years. How much more in accord with this old lady's truth it was to say, 'He's very close to you just now.'

Eric Rayner, in his book *Human Development*, describes how our highly integrated thought processes can break down in extreme old age and more primitive mental functions then emerge. He has written: 'The primitive symbolism of a senile person can often however be deciphered by a listener. When this is achieved, the contact between him and the old person can be very moving for both.'[4] He gives an example of an abstract idea being expressed in terms of bodily functions. A listener who knows the old person well can usually translate what is being communicated:

An old man was clouded and wandering in his mind. His son came to ask for his signature for a power of attorney to manage affairs, and was worried whether his father would understand and comply. The old man seemed to wander off to another subject when he said, 'I must climb on your shoulders. I hope I won't be too heavy.' The son, realizing what he meant, said, 'Oh no, everything is in order and we shall be able to manage things quite well', and then handed him pen and paper. His father signed it and, with a sigh, said, 'That's much more comfortable now, but then you always were a broad shouldered boy'.[5]

Rayner is a Freudian. He gives here no definition of selfhood, but sees how a person's external and internal reality can become confused, as it does in dreams, in psychosis, and also in early infancy:

> In adult life we use our inner phantasy to feed our creative imagination in relation to the outside world. Then with senility the differentiation breaks down and we can communicate only through concrete symbolic language very like the imagery of dreams. Perhaps as people become more sensitive to primitive symbolic communication, the loneliness of old and senile people will be somewhat alleviated.[6]

A story is told by a priest visiting an Alzheimer case in hospital. She was sitting quietly in her wheelchair. At his first 'Hello' she pounded the side of her chair and screamed at him, 'Who's taking care of that baby? Why isn't someone doing something for that baby?' He sat down and tried to work out what she was trying to say. Which baby? He thought of blaming the television and the soap opera going on in front of her. He began to get annoyed that we set confused people in front of all this noise on 'the idiot box' in a misguided attempt to calm them. But the baby was not on the television. On the far side of the room, another old lady, also chairbound, was screaming for her mother and no one was responding:

> So I spoke to Harriet about her mothering, her own sense of the importance of children. . . . She calmed down. . . . When I sensed our conversation was coming to an end, I suggested to Harriet that perhaps I should go over and help the child crying for her mother. She thought that was a splendid idea and as I got up to leave she said, 'Now you come back and visit me again.'[7]

It seems that, after all, the barriers between the 'strange states' of dementia and our own familiar territory are not totally impassable, unless we are so prejudiced that we are only able to listen to one language. The priest visiting Harriet enjoyed these visits because they freed him from the need to be exact about things. He said: 'We live in a very rational world — people want to know what time it is — they want to know where they are going next — all those things that you and I worry about. I often find that with the confused you can chat heart to heart. You can touch people where we really come together.'8

When approaching death, people move into a state of timelessness and yet sometimes they may know more than we, who watch them, about what is going to happen. One demented person who had behaved (seemingly) like a vegetable for weeks on end, suddenly opened her eyes one day in October and announced, 'Boxing Day.' She said no more, but on Boxing Day she died. Another old lady, whose speech had been locked up for years with Parkinson's disease, responded to her obviously tired daughter's 'Are you all right, Mother?' with a clear, 'Provided *you* are not all wrong.' She was over a hundred and very near to death, but more aware of what was going on inside her than many people realized.

All through this book, we keep coming up against paradox and this pertains both to ageing and to dying. We have seen how the very old need the loving care that we seem to give more readily to the very young, how they need to be respected for the fullness of their lives, and that how even those written off as senile can sometimes speak words of wisdom. We need to respect both their living and their dying.

People worry about their manner of dying. Some would prefer it to happen at a time of their own choosing. And so we have to face the thorny problem of euthanasia. A plea to the doctor or relative to 'end it all' should not always be interpreted as a wish to die. The sufferer is certainly begging for an end to pain, and perhaps death seems the only way, but there may well be an underlying cry for help, for some magic elixir that brings life, not death. If this is the case, what needs to be given is help in letting that person die with acceptance, peace, dignity and the minimum of physical pain. If strong drugs are given to relieve pain, they may in fact hasten death, but we do not usually equate this hastening with euthanasia; the latter involves deliberate killing, however gently undertaken and however humanitarian the motive. Some people long for death to come quickly and may advocate the legalizing of euthanasia, and even ask for themselves a secret 'mercy-killing'. There are others who would rather face their own dying in full consciousness without drugs. Either choice needs to be respected. Both may be hard to carry out.

Suicide is no longer a crime. The Samaritans, recognizing that humans have the gift of free will, do not, although making every effort at dissuasion, forcibly interfere with an individual's declared wish — or not until loss of consciousness puts an end to choice, and by then the rescue may be too late. If that person's life is saved, there may, or may not, be gratitude. That 'may or may not' is an important phrase. There is no certainty that anyone's choice at one moment will be lasting. People's views on euthanasia tend to be ambivalent. Unlike suicide, another person's help has to be enlisted, for when it comes to the 'right' moment the sufferer will probably be past reaching for the fatal dose. A nurse at St Christopher's hospice described a typical case of how the desire for choice fluctuates:

> 'If I ever get like that chap, I'd want to do something to myself.' In fact, when he finally reached almost exactly the same condition in his turn, he found that his feelings had changed and that the experience from inside was not what it appeared to the onlooker . . . 'I can't see round the next bend but I know I'll be all right.' He found, as he said, that what he had experienced and what he had seen in others was a 'bringing-together' illness. In this kind of life the complexities fall away; what is left is what matters.[9]

However humanitarian it might seem to shorten a period of suffering, who is to judge the extent to which we may rob a person of an important experience? And, indeed, one wonders whether this is in fact quite frequently done through over-medication. When onlookers witness what they describe as 'a peaceful death' or even that cliché, 'a merciful release', who, one may ask, is being saved from suffering: the dying person or those in attendance? To others, the passing looks like a struggle. T. S. Eliot used the words 'hard and bitter agony' in his poem 'The Voyage of the Magi', in which he uses the phrase for both death and birth; having seen both, he thought they were different. Those few who come back to life from near-death experiences describe something like a hint of new birth at the point of death. But, like labour, there must first be pain. Some dying people have a 'joyful vocation to suffering' and refuse sedation. They know that God is with them even if they are too weak to pray: '. . . but we just lie back in his arms and that is prayer. . . . That is the only thing.'[10]

Sometimes we have unexpected glimpses of joy or surprise at the moment of death, and occasionally this is expressed in words. 'Am I dead?' asked one old lady, waking suddenly. The next moment she died with a murmur of 'How glorious!' Another, who had also seemed asleep, sat bolt upright with an astonished 'Ah!' Then she lay down and died with a smile on her face.

The debate about euthanasia continues and there are no imminent signs of it being legalized in Britain. If doctors are occasionally prepared to practise mercy-killing, they tend not to declare it publicly, but many would not bring themselves to break the Hippocratic oath and their vocation to cure. However, allowing a natural death is a different question. Pneumonia, popularly known as 'the old man's friend', is often left untreated, especially in cases of terminal cancer or extreme old age. Often this is agreed with the patient beforehand. Life-support machines get turned off when 'brain death' has already replaced meaningful life. But this is not done lightly and there is often an agony of soul-searching before making such a final decision. A lot of us would agree with the poet Clough, who back in the nineteenth century wrote: 'Thou shalt not kill; but needs't not strive/Officiously to keep alive.' But what he advocates is a far cry from euthanasia.

Probably all of us are afraid of dying. No one accepts easily the anticipation of pain, loss of control, being totally dependent on others, becoming a burden and a nuisance and perhaps, most of all, saying goodbye to the familiar world and all the people we like and love. Fear of death — as a state of the body's dissolution and simply not being alive — is different and harder to talk about. It has little, or nothing, to do with ageing. Some are dogged all their lives with this particular dread, sometimes known as 'ontological anxiety'. Of these two fears, the first is the most universal, but one or other is nearly always strong enough for us to work hard, throughout life, at building up defence mechanisms, either against the process of dying or death itself.

Until recently, our society, in sharp contrast to the Victorians, has managed considerable avoidance of the subject of death. This has a lot to do with advances in medicine, lower infant mortality, smaller families and people dying in hospital, out of sight. Doctors have too often come to see death as a medical failure. They have been taught to cure, not to let people die.

Those getting older today have lived with this avoidance and are likely to have memories of being left in ignorance about sudden disappearances of their older relatives (often much loved grandparents), of being sent away to stay with friends to avoid funeral arrangements and, hardly ever, except perhaps in the case of actual parents, attending a funeral or seeing a dead body. Denial of death goes together with the waning of conventional hope in an afterlife, although most non-believers have tended to have Christian funerals. These have often been of the conveyor-belt variety, joining the queue in the crematorium for a fifteen-minute travesty of a ceremony conducted by a stranger. But the taboo is slowly lifting; today, the unbeliever has more choice and is able to organize a humanistic type of funeral, which celebrates the dead person's life with no pretence at a religious dimension. This, at least, is honest. On the other hand, there are more agnostics among us than atheists and these shaky half-believers are many of them nominal Christians, baptized in infancy. Who knows whether the traditional words of hope — 'I am the resurrection and the life', or the well-known comfort of the twenty-third psalm — may evoke in some of them intimations of mysteries beyond the ordinary and the familiar?

However short or bleak the funeral, memorial services,

once reserved for famous figures, are becoming more usual; these are opportunities, after the first pangs of grief have subsided, to celebrate a dead friend's life in a personal way, through memories, music, poetry and perhaps a bit of humour. They are occasions when boundaries between religion and secularity merge and no one is likely to be offended.

Death, at last, is being talked about and the defences are breaking down. In most towns there is a hospice, built purposely for the dying: a place where the staff are geared to relieve pain rather than to cure, where facts of terminal illness are faced with honesty, and questions of life and death are not brushed aside.

How usual it seems to be, particularly between married couples, that an agreement is made earlier in life to face the truth together when the time comes for one or other to die; and yet, how usual also that when death becomes certain, the agreement is broken and everyone acts a lie. A new attitude, though, fostered by the hospice movement and Macmillan nurses, is helping us all to face the truth about dying and to attend to individual fears.

To tell or not to tell has always been the question. If both doctors and priests advise against telling — and this has only too often been the case in the past — it is hard for relatives to go against their professional advice. And this seems to apply even when the dying person has expressed in advance a strong desire not to be kept in the dark when death is known to be inescapable. All too often, the earlier promises get broken and no respect is shown for a person's courage and responsibility in facing *the* most important of life's transitions.

Once we decide to tell, attention must be given as to how this should be done and who should do the telling. Doctors, as we have already mentioned, are inclined to see death as a failure that they find hard to admit. They have in the past taken the line that telling the truth will make a patient worse, thus giving themselves an excuse to avoid this unpleasant task. Even in today's climate, some find it almost impossible (even when asked by the nearest relative to tell the patient the truth). Sometimes they get the timing wrong so that they make the announcement abruptly before the patient is ready to hear it, or else wrap up the truth in such medical terminology as to make it unintelligible.

This is not, of course, true of all doctors, especially those trained since the hospice movement came into being. But what still needs attention is the doctor's sense of failure at not producing a magic cure. Now that the average life-span has extended quite dramatically, it may seem to some that we are on the verge of postponing death indefinitely. For such medical optimists, the incurability of AIDS, together with environmental hazards beyond our control, must be a humbling experience. In the last chapter, we looked at the stress suffered by those in caring positions. And by 'carers' we meant all those involved with old age and death — doctors, priests, nurses, assistants, as well as those close relatives who usually take most responsibility and do the hardest work.

Some years ago, a wife had to struggle with how to tell her husband he was dying. We will call the couple Charles and Kate. Charles was in his late sixties and had some discomfort from arthritis but was otherwise healthy, had a lively mind and gave the impression of being younger than his years. The first symptom was heart failure, followed by disorientation and vertigo. He was advised to lose weight and the heart condition, which was not considered serious, was treated, only to return within a week or so. In hospital, no one seemed to notice his increasing mental vagueness, till at last the heart specialist, who had enjoyed talking and joking with him as one human being to another, agreed with Kate that something abnormal was going on. 'At worst,' he said, 'he might have had a slight stroke.' It was decided to give him a brain scan; Kate was told not to worry, but to telephone the doctor late the next day. Before she could get to the telephone, Charles rang himself to say that he had been given good news — some slight trouble with his arteries, but easily treatable. Relieved, but still with some trepidation, Kate rang the doctor at the agreed time. She was alone in the house. 'Are you sitting down?' said the doctor, 'I'm afraid I have very bad news.' Charles had secondary cancer, widespread in his brain. 'Then — there's nothing you can do?' asked Kate. The doctor spoke gently to her. 'Short term, we can help him quite a lot. You'll notice the difference almost at once.'

Next day she saw the doctor before visiting Charles and told him that she did not want any secrets. 'I don't usually tell people,' he said, 'but I'm willing to do whatever you like. What do you want me to say to him?' 'The truth,' was her reply. She went up to Charles's room. 'It's good news, isn't it?' He greeted her eagerly, then looked at her hard. 'But why do you seem so strained?' All she could bring herself to say was that the doctor was coming to tell him that his condition would be harder to treat than first anticipated. 'Am I going to die?' asked Charles. Kate was so startled that she could not give him a direct answer, but repeated what she had already said. The doctor joined them and explained to Charles that he had a tumour and would be given some drugs and radiotherapy. Charles gave no sign of paying attention. Kate asked if he had heard what had just been said. 'Oh yes — I've some sort of growth and they're going to put electricity through my brain.' He seemed unperturbed.

That same day, Kate telephoned a friend who had been a GP and was now a psychotherapist. He gave her two bits of advice, 'for what they're worth', he said. One was not to tell lies, the other was not to answer questions before they were asked. She had already undone the lies, and now she waited for the questions. These were very direct but unexpected, and she found herself hedging more than she had intended. Charles, who had no interest in medicine, never asked about the diagnosis. But in the evening of that first day he asked, 'Will this shorten my life?' 'Yes,' said Kate, relieved at giving a straight, truthful answer. He wanted to know by how much. 'Will it be next week or in twenty-five years?' Kate was able to smile. 'Well, judging by the age you are now, even without an illness, it would be likely to be some time between the two.'

So he gave himself an arbitrary seven years and she did not contradict him. The doctor had mentioned no definite time. It could be weeks or months. All that was certain was that his mental powers would deteriorate. Kate was aware of there not being much time left for communication.

Meanwhile there was a marked improvement. During the course of treatment, Charles was allowed home for weekends and then eventually discharged, with the promise that he could be readmitted if necessary. Kate was determined that, whatever it cost, Charles would die in his own home. His mind seemed clear, though he got increasingly sleepy. Then gradually he became paralysed, and eventually needed full-time nursing. He assured Kate that he was not afraid of dying. 'I feel a burden has been lifted,' then added regretfully, 'and put on to you.' He kept reassuring her (or was he reassuring himself?), 'You'll be all right.' She kept repeating, 'Yes, I'll be all right.'

After he had died, she wished she had shown more of the anguish that she felt and her terror of losing him as a strong person on whom she had for so long been dependent. At the time, she did not dare say anything that would make things worse for him, but sometimes this felt like not telling him how much she loved him. She kept remembering how little time they had and dreaded living with him after he had deteriorated, expecting an indefinite period of vegetable existence. As it was, they had two months, knowing the truth. Towards the end, he spoke less and slept more. His only anxiety about dying was that it might be undignified. His imagined life-span became shorter as he got used to coping with his finiteness, but sometimes he forgot and made plans for the future. He often said, 'We'll spend Christmas together, won't we?' But he died in October. A few weeks before, Kate pushed him into asking what illness he had, and at last he said, 'Is it cancer?' His only comment was, 'Well, if I've got cancer of the brain, of course I can't drive a car.' He died of pneumonia which, as agreed beforehand, was not treated with antibiotics. There was time, while still more or less conscious, for him to receive the last rites. He was anointed, then seemed to sleep. 'Do you want your communion, Charles?' 'Yes.' This was said in a clear voice. He had a strong belief, but had never seen much point in the sacraments.

After he died, Kate wondered if she had been right in sticking so rigidly to the advice about answering questions and wished she had taken some initiative herself in talking about death and sharing the experience. There were no visits from Macmillan nurses. Staff in the hospital saw him off with cheery platitudes about getting well soon. The GP was able to have some talk with him about dying and to promise him that it would be painless, but somehow he never managed to say much to Kate. When she thought back to her father's death fourteen years before, Kate remembered how much she had wanted to tell him that he was going to die, but everyone advised against it and her mother followed professional advice. Charles, she realized, had died more peacefully than her father.

Ninety-five-year-old Mike, sitting upright and smartly dressed with collar and tie, receives his visitors with courtesy and apologies for not being able to stand up. Straight away he says what the trouble is. He is clear about it himself and wants others to know. 'I've got a bad cancer in the prostate. My liver's in a mess and now it's gone to the bones. But there isn't any pain.' His room at the hospice is light and sunny with French windows, big enough for a bed to be wheeled into the garden. He was worried earlier this year when there had been a misdiagnosis and he was given the wrong medication. Now, he feels everything is under control — everything that is, except that no one can tell him the date of his death, just that it might be any time.

Mike is a survivor. He has come through two world wars, the first in a field ambulance unit (he saw the Battle of the Somme), the second as a firefighter in the London blitz. He saw plenty of bloodshed, but was never wounded himself. 'Death? We never thought about it — too busy. There was a lot of laughter in the trenches. Mind you, I spent my time mopping up other people's wounds. The first thing was to get them cleaned up. They didn't look so bad then.' He was a pharmacist by profession and interested in anything medical. He got an untrained soldier — 'hefty fellow' — to pull out one of his badly aching teeth. 'Pain? Of course there was pain, but I'd been brought up to bear it. Self-control, duty, honour — those are the important things. That's what freemasonry is all about. My family was non-conformist, very strict, but — being a mason, that's my religion now.' He has refused to see a minister from his own denomination, but has talks sometimes with the vicar in whose parish the hospice belongs. He likes the Bible — but only the King James version — and especially the Sermon on the Mount. He has no belief in an afterlife, which he can only see in purely material form as a rather overcrowded place — 'so it must be nonsense'. And anyway, there are a great many people he has no wish to see again. One wonders about his wife who is still alive and the same age as himself, but he is satisfied that she will be looked after. While waiting to die, he feels relieved that he has left everything in good order. His will is fair and his possessions properly shared out among his children, grand-children and great grandchildren. Last week he celebrated his seventieth wedding anniversary with the whole family present. They came from all over England. There was a telegram from the Queen and the hospice laid on a party. The staff had feared that he might not live to see it, but, perhaps buoyed up by the event, he is having a period of remission, enjoying his food and talking to people. He enjoys day-to-day happenings and is appreciative of the kindness and honesty of his carers, but through most of our conversation he showed little emotion. He has had a good innings and nothing seems to matter any more. It was when he described the anniversary party that enthusiasm came into his voice and he looked, just for a moment, near to tears. 'When you get very old, your emotions are close to the surface,' he said. Then his common sense prevailed. 'I think the hospice liked giving the party — for the publicity, you know — but they're good people. They've been straight with me. When they say that I'll die without pain, I believe them.' 'Not so much pain as that tooth being pulled out in the trenches,' said his visitor. He smiled and repeated again that he had no worries at all about dying.

Twenty years have passed between Kate's father's death in agitated ignorance and Mike facing his dying serenely, knowing the worst that could happen to him. In this new era of honesty, several writers have spelt out clearly certain psychological stages or reactions that are supposedly common to those who know they will die soon. These are similar to the stages of bereavement, already described in an earlier chapter. The work of Kübler-Ross has been particularly influential in this area. First, in a state of shock, people are seen to defend themselves by *denial*. This gives way to *anger*. Why me? Then they move on to *bargaining* — with the doctors or with God. As defences break down, a quite realistic *depression* may be expected, the obvious reaction to any loss. And this, in turn, gives way to *acceptance*. But, as in bereavement, we cannot expect one stage to follow the other in neat succession and certainly not everyone dies with serene acceptance. Those who fight their illnesses are often admired. Dylan Thomas addressed a poem to his father: 'Do not go gently into that good night./Rage, rage against the dying of the light.' It is not always easy to see the difference between giving up too early and realizing that the fight is useless — that, in other words, there is an important difference between resignation and acceptance. A friend of Charles (who, as just described, lived through his last days serenely) said to Kate, 'Why doesn't he show more fight?' Her reply was, 'Because he knows there's no point. Don't discourage him from accepting his death.'

'Only patients who have been able to work through their anguish and anxieties are able to achieve this stage. Sometimes people get stuck and reach a point where they don't live and don't die, this is often seen in geriatric nursing homes.'[11] Each person's dying is unique. Cicely Saunders is quoted as having said, 'They should be helped to die in the same individual way in which they have lived.'[12]

Each person has a different fear. So far we have looked at reactions to the process of dying, rather than fear of what happens (or does *not* happen) afterwards. For many older Christians, this fear is of something quite concrete — judgement and hell. This has been touched upon already in our chapter on pastoral visiting. One need look no further than the Book of Common Prayer — on which so many of the older generation have been brought up — to notice (or remember) the emphasis on God's wrath, which some have heard preached at them from childhood, almost to the point of obliterating God's love. As for mercy, it was something pleaded for in so many prayers that God was not seen as dispensing it very readily. If the dying are surrounded by loving human beings, and if they can be told repeatedly of God's love, so plainly evident in the Christian Gospels, let us hope that this particular fear can be dispelled.

Fear of something, even fear of hell fire and a host of devils, often covers a much deeper fear of nothingness. Christians and non-Christians alike often suffer this particular dread, one that has no images, for images turn it into fear of something, and from something one may imagine a way of escape. The deepest fears are of annihilation and ultimate abandonment, which are closely linked with fear of the unknown. And this must carry with it the realization that neither death nor the meaning of life can be contained in human consciousness. Indeed, if this were possible, the knowledge would be so limited as to be worth nothing. Not knowing, therefore, is necessary and healthy.

Several writers have tried to imagine beings who live for ever. Swift's Struldbrugs in *Gulliver's Travels* were given the doubtful privilege of immortality without eternal strength or intellect to cope with it. And thus they were condemned to life and longed to die. Unending life, in the only way we can know it, would involve endless repetition and no moving on. The Lotus Eaters, in Homeric legend, were given endless ease and luxury and found themselves stuck, according to Tennyson, in a land where it was always afternoon.

It comes naturally to most of us to think of life as a journey and that we are striving to reach a goal, even if we never fully know our destiny. Jung was convinced that our goal is death, and that, unconsciously, we, along with the whole of nature, prepare for it right through our lives. 'Death is psychologically as important as birth and, like it, is an integral part of life.'[13] Without death, life would have no shape, hence the aimlessness of the Struldbrugs.

Stepping into the unknown is an adventure. Some dread it; some long for it. When the very old have gradually stripped themselves of all meaningful aspects of life, when they at last get very tired and let themselves forget what it is no longer important to remember, some at least can look forward easily, if not eagerly, to death as a goal.

However unknown our destiny, perhaps we can hope with St Paul: 'Eye hath not seen, nor ear heard, neither have entered into the heart of man, the things which God hath prepared for them that love Him' (1 Corinthians 2.9).

Notes

1. C. J. Gilleard, *Living with Dementia*, Croom Helm 1984, p. 18.
2. ibid., p. 20.
3. S. Harton, *On Growing Old*, Hodder & Stoughton 1957.
4. E. H. Rayner, *Human Development: An Introduction to the Psychodynamics of Growth, Maturity and Ageing*, Allen & Unwin 1978, p. 242.
5. ibid., p. 243.
6. ibid.
7. H. R. Nevel, 'Spiritual Care of the Frail Elderly', in *Plus: quarterly journal of the Christian Council of Ageing*, Spring 1989.
8. ibid.
9. S. Gamsu, 'A Will to Live', in *St Christopher's in Celebration*, Hodder & Stoughton 1984.
10. G. Barfoot, *The Witness of Edith Barfoot*, Basil Blackwell 1977.
11. J. Doran, 'Death and Dying — A Message for the Living', unpublished project for Chichester Counselling Services.
12. ibid.
13. C. G. Jung, quoted in R. Wilhelm, *Secret of the Golden Flower: Chinese Book of Life*, Routledge 1962.

TWELVE

The Spiritual Journey

When we grow old, everything leaves us.
But God comes.
René Bazin

What do people mean by 'spirituality'? Many churchgoers
have a very narrow view of its meaning, assuming it has to do
with regular attendance, singing in the choir, sitting on the
PCC and perhaps doing some pastoral work, which might
even include visiting the old. But, as we have seen in Chapters
8 and 9, visiting and counselling are not tasks to be taken up
lightly, but in a spirit of humility, openness and mutual self-
awareness. On both sides, there needs to be an exploration of
the meaning of life, otherwise there will just be an empty, or
even antagonistic, exchange of views. Each person's spirituality is unique, but that does not mean it cannot be shared. We
have looked at the agony and loneliness that ensues when
carers, and those they care for, get locked together in prisons
that they make for each other, through an inability to
empathize with their different ways of being. We need, at all
ages, an extra 'spiritual dimension' to our lives if we are to
bridge the gaps of generation, race, culture or sex. But what
is this elusive dimension? The *Concise Oxford Dictionary* is
misleadingly concise! This is all it offers us in its definition of
'spirituality': 'What belongs or is due to the Church . . .'.
Surprisingly, the *Oxford Dictionary of the Christian Church*
has nothing to say by way of definition.

We would have to be extraordinarily bigoted, living as we
do today in a multi-cultural society, to turn a blind eye to the
spirituality of non-churchgoers. If we look again at Jung,

whom we have turned to for much spiritual guidance in the course of this book, he was from an early age aware of God in his life: 'Nobody could rob me of the conviction that it was enjoined on me to do what God wanted and not what I wanted.'[1] But, as a Swiss pastor's son, he could find no enrichment in his father's practice of Christianity, in which he found creed without experience. 'Why, that is not religion at all. It is an absence of God: the Church is a place I should not go to. It is not life which is there, but death.'[2] These are strong words and bring home to us how much the Church must have failed in its relevance to a number of intensely spiritual people. If this failure is to be repaired, church workers certainly need to be clearer about what constitutes true spirituality, both outside and inside Christian practice.

First, and most important, is the need to know who we are, and this applies to all ages; however, as we have seen, a sense of identity may be particularly in danger of getting lost in old people, through bodily change, memory loss, the loss of friends through death, and thus having no one with whom to share the story of their lives. It is this life story and the sense of continuity which comes through being able to recount it, that needs affirming again and again. This will include going over bad as well as good experiences, having permission to share — and thereby hope to heal — old wounds, and being helped to forgive both oneself and others. Forgiveness of those who are dead certainly requires a spiritual dimension. 'Healing of the Memories' is a term often used for the mourning and letting go of past failures, so as to entrust to God the patchwork of joy/sorrow, love/hate, success/error and, in fact, all the opposites through which a person has struggled in a long life. 'Let go and let God' is not an admonition, but a simple prayer for release.

Giving value to ourselves — 'liking being me' — so that we can give value to others, makes for spiritual well-being in that we recognize the value we have ourselves been given. A lot of this value came in the past from parents, friends and lovers. We may not always recognize it as God-given, but in old age, when so many of our old loves have been taken away, we would do well to acknowledge that we are in touch with something beyond our finite humanity, whether or not we give this anchorhold the name of God. Spirituality is not properly assessed by the words through which people communicate their experience of it, and Christian helpers need to keep their ears well tuned to an assortment of languages and stories.

The metaphor of a journey through life is ages old. Legends, fairy stories, the Quest for the Holy Grail, Dante's explorations of hell and heaven, *The Pilgrim's Progress, Paradise Lost* and *Paradise Regained* — all these reiterate themes of being lost and found, and of many strivings on the way to reach a longed-for goal. Eliot's *Four Quartets* take us from the rose garden, where we hear children's laughter in 'our first world', to which it seems we only return when we stop nostalgically looking back: 'Down the passage which we did not take/ Towards the door we never opened.' In order to arrive, we must first descend into 'internal darkness'. This reminds us of the psychological journey (Jung's 'Individuation') that we take in order to explore the repressed parts of our psyches, aspects of ourselves we are tempted to leave alone. It means struggling with contradictions. 'What you do not know is the only thing you know/And what you own is what you do not own/And where you are is where you are not.' Till, at last, 'I said to my soul, be stilled and let the dark come upon you/which shall be the darkness of God.'[3]

That stillness must surely be every old person's goal.

Youth is a time for looking forward, and limitless opportunities beckon. There are no horizons in sight. In middle age, we begin to realize our finiteness and we sort out priorities in work and relationships. Some of our earlier dreams must be dropped, but not without sadness. We continue the journey with fewer, but more realistic, hopes. We still carry a great deal of luggage, much of it unnecessary, and still we get distracted into byways before finally letting God take over and guide us. The old who cannot find serenity are those who go on fighting for control. Seniority and parenthood are hard to relinquish and these old fighters, just as much as their chairbound or dementing contemporaries, can sometimes make life hell for their carers.

Serenity does not mean opting out of life, but it does necessitate more *being* and less *doing*. We saw, in Chapter 4 on retirement, how easily a person becomes identified with his career. How much healthier it would be to say 'I am teaching' than 'I am a teacher'; the former carries the implication that, 'I am teaching this year. Next year I may be writing, reading or simply basking in the sun.' The job is not the person; it is simply what that person does during part of his life story. For those who mistake 'do-gooding' and churchgoing for spirituality, it might be salutary for them to say something like: 'I do Meals on Wheels every Monday because I believe I am performing a necessary service and one that I have the ability to do. Also I like to be greeted with smiles, and I have a knack of getting old people to like me. I enjoy the fellowship of the Christian family and look forward to our meetings together on Sundays. I like the beauty of the church service, the music and flower arrangements.' Perhaps this person also feels able to talk to God, especially if there are formal prayers to hear and remember. Being silent may feel uncomfortable to some — even though the Quakers learn to be happy with it from childhood — and few Anglican services allow time for silence, busy as they are fitting as much as possible into a short time. To go over the prescribed hour would probably invite criticism.

But the old move at a slower pace. Are our church services geared to meet their special needs? Are the older members even welcomed? One priest is reported to have moaned: 'My parish is stacked with old people. You won't find a young person attending that church. They're all wrinklies.'

A young, lively congregation is what every priest longs for; it creates a good impression. He will be congratulated on bridging the generation gap, for adapting his form of worship, perhaps with guitars and pop tunes, to a new generation. He is seen as getting the young 'involved', in the hope that they will stay long enough to bring their children to be 'involved' in turn. But what of those already involved, those who in their old age might like a little less noise, more dignity and more silence? They are prepared to do some adapting to changing habits, but nevertheless they feel some nostalgia for the traditions in which they were brought up.

The fact remains that these are the 'old faithfuls' who form the greater part of most congregations. But how often are they ever consulted, unless they are bold enough to push themselves forward and take the risk of being laughed at or 'jollied along'? 'Oh come on, Mrs Jones. You must move with the times. You're as young as you feel.' The point that Mrs Jones will probably never get a chance to make — because the priest has turned away to welcome a younger newcomer — is that she is as *old* as she feels and only too glad to give up a mock youthfulness.

On the practical level, we might learn from the religious orders who, because they are eager for their older members to join them for worship, have seen to it that there is both easy access for wheelchairs and good apparatus to amplify the sound — not of jazz and guitars, but the quieter parts of the service. Old people's needs could be met more easily if it were happily acknowledged that they make up the bulk of most congregations. One would not want to deny occasions for the young to have fun in church, but other services might be geared specially for the old. Not only do they want to be quieter, but they also want to be more comfortable. Standing for the prayer of consecration, or during long anthems, should not be so much the norm that older people are ashamed to sit. Popping up and down on creaky joints is tiring, but, once sitting is allowed, perhaps the pews, or preferably chairs, could be made more enticing. There might also be more trouble taken over encouraging older people to sit in the front, so that they have less of a trek to the communion rail. They do not want to be made conspicuous, provided they can still walk, by having communion brought to their pews — although this may be necessary in some cases.

A workshop attended by clergy and secular agencies grappled with the concept of a 'spiritual dimension', and explored how, when we use such terms as 'low in spirit' (as indeed we also say 'high spirited'), we are making a link with a person's individual religious values and beliefs. Many of the same conclusions emerged as those already mentioned in this chapter and earlier in the book. It was decided that spirituality had to do with meaning and purpose, and appreciation of the non-material world, the state of 'inner being' (peace and self-worth), freedom from fear and guilt, the need to belong and the need to grow. What role, the participants wondered, could the Church play in being open with people and able to discuss spiritual issues. While sometimes the 'authority' of the clergy could be threatening rather than encouraging, its representatives were likely to be the chief helpers to their actual congregations. The secular professions were assured that any befriending of non-churchgoers by the Christian pastoral workers would not include a 'hard-sell', but that it would be expected that a person's relationship with God would implicitly, if not always overtly, be affecting his or her perception of the world and relationship with others.

In cases of isolation, the Church could do a lot of befriending if a lonely person were able to be introduced to appropriate parish activities. Where there was found to be bitterness, resentment and guilt, healing might be possible through pastoral visits or counselling. We have already discussed this issue at some length. We have also mentioned two different fears: fear of the process of dying, and death itself as annihilation. And these fears can be present both in believers and non-believers.

Several times in this book we have mentioned people who are angry with God. The workshop mentioned above thought it important that there should be reconciliation. It seems that this anger first needs to be acknowledged, without shame. People who have suffered extreme misfortune have, in the authors' view, a right to be angry. If this anger is vented against the Church, a reinclusion into church life (which the workshop recommended) may not be easy to bring about. Likewise, when it comes to forgiveness, this cannot be forced. One rabbi, leading prayers at a memorial day in the camp of Auschwitz, was asked by a priest why he had not prayed for the perpetrators of the crimes. Were we not supposed to forgive our enemies? The rabbi replied, quite humbly, that this was something he could not bring himself to do. His religious practice did not necessarily enjoin him to forgive such tremendous wrong. Only God, he said, had the power to forgive. Perhaps — and not unreasonably — he found it difficult to forgive God. Accepting his weakness, he was as reconciled as it was possible to be in such extreme circumstances. He left the rest to God.

In tackling depression and a sense of meaninglessness, visiting and counselling have a big part to play. Within the Church, new outlets may be found for a person to give his or her unique contribution and to find that gift valued. Church contact must always revitalize and bring new interests, rather than offering something stale and repetitive:

> It is important that the churches clarify what they can offer; not only through the clergy, but also from their congregation, in terms of type of help and whether it is likely to be long or short-term. The clergy were also asked to look at their worship; to what extent any ritual gets in the way, or enhances the opportunities for acceptance and fellowship of those who could feel excluded by, for example, their inability to read (including poor eyesight) . . . value is seen in Church involvement alongside the secular workers: churches being not only the place [sic] where religious needs can be met, but where Christians could be expected to add an 'extra dimension' to practical help through an ability and willingness to enter into, be sensitive to, the 'spiritual' searchings and experiences of life for each individual. It is important that church congregations as well as clergy are aware of these expectations by secular professionals and the opportunity and responsibility they present.[4]

These words would seem to sum up most of what we have been discussing in the last few pages.

Yet there is an intensely private side to each person's spirituality, and much of its inward growth is unconscious. There are limits to how much this growth can be forced by the conscious will, and the efforts of outsiders, however worthy their intentions, can all too easily be clumsy and ill-timed. That is why, in the last resort, waiting, listening and simply being with a person is both the best and only help that any befriender can give. What is really going on in the 'soul making' of any individual is infinitely mysterious and may never be expressed in words. Some, whom we may even have written off as demented, surprise us by their last words when dying. Perhaps they also surprise themselves, but that is a secret that we shall never know. Paul Tournier, the Swiss psychiatrist, reports on two dying patients whose last words were, 'I'm going to know.'[5] These patients had great faith and could perhaps picture a world beyond this one and the voice of Christ talking to them. But might there be an even greater faith in that total surrender to God, a surrender without expectations, not even of knowledge, and yet where there can still be trust? As one professed unbeliever was heard to say, 'I'm ready to fit in with the arrangements, whatever they may turn out to be.' And another, this time a Christian voice: 'If God wants me to be no more than a bit of shit, then I'll be a happy bit of shit.' This last comment may sound shocking, but it was experienced by the dying person as the ultimate breakthrough of self-giving.

There comes a time when there is no choice between doing and being. Stripped, as it were, to the bare bones of physical living, what is left is soul. And soul — or whatever other name we care to call it — can still grow, even though other faculties dwindle.

There is no point in being in a hurry. If death, as Jung says, is 'psychologically as important as birth . . . an integral part of life',[6] one can assume it to have a period of gestation, akin to pregnancy. Neither the foetus nor the person at the other end of the journey has conscious knowledge of this growth, yet both beginning and ending are natural processes and, unconsciously, we prepare for them.

As Teilhard de Chardin wrote:

There is no need to be wildly impatient. The master of death will come soon enough — and perhaps we can already hear his footsteps. There is no need to forestall his hour nor to fear it. When he enters into us to destroy, as it seems, the virtues of the forces that we have distilled with so much loving care out of the sap of the world, it will be a loving fire to consummate our completion in union.[7]

The very old have to give up pursuing one-sided goals. Building up the ego, once necessary for achievement, is pointless now. Even striving for the good of one's children, after making wills and leaving material things in order, has at last to be relinquished. As for one's sins, probably, through patient waiting, many of the earlier temptations fall away. According to Jung, people grow beyond themselves. 'What, on a lower level, had led to the wildest conflicts and to panicky outbursts of emotion, from the higher level of personality now looked like a storm seen from the mountain top. This does not mean that the storm is robbed of its reality, but instead of being in it one is above it.'[8] This mountain top may sound an impossible ideal, but he goes on to say that the change that occurs, the 'new thing', was, in the cases where he saw it grow, not 'conjured into existence intentionally or by conscious willing, but rather seemed to be borne along on the stream of time'.[9] We need to distinguish between this unconscious growing beyond ourselves and the unrealistic striving of the will, which would turn this same phrase into the sort of situation in which one would say of a person that he is 'big-headed' or 'too big for his boots'. The ideal that Jung describes has a lot to do with being prepared to be ordinary. One sixty-year-old who had been a perfectionist all her life and had fantasies of being responsible for all the troubles of the world, came at last to realize that she needed to come to terms with being an 'imperfect person'. She was reminded that she also had to live in an imperfect world with no absolute certainties to which she could cling. The certainty of a perfect heaven beyond this life is an essential ingredient in many people's faith, but quite unimaginable to others. Yet many can die in doubt and still be serene, accepting that death is a natural, and therefore ordinary, process; and that in this ordinariness there is order, and therefore meaning, in the universe.

This ordinariness is well summed up by George Eliot, who ends her novel *Middlemarch* with these words: '. . . for the growing good of the world is partly dependent on unhistoric acts: and that things are not so ill with you and me as they might have been, is half owing to the number who lived faithfully, a hidden life, and rest in unvisited tombs'.[10]

There seems to be some sort of expectation among Christians that these ordinary old people have extraordinary powers in their capacity for prayer, the implication being that, since they are not much good for anything else, at least they can pray for us. So, before we leave them in their 'unvisited tombs', it may be worth trying to catch a glimpse of them at prayer. Perhaps we will be disappointed to find that age is not in itself a badge of sanctity, and a lot of old people's prayers are no more special than those of anyone else.

As yet, there is no broad-based investigation into older people's prayer life. The Reverend Graham Keyes of St Hilda's, Jesmond, Newcastle, made a study of six individuals, all of whom were retired: five women and one man. Two were housebound, and the others were physically active. According to the WEISS Scale, two were 'rather isolated' and two were definitely 'isolated'. Prior to retirement, they followed a variety of occupations, mostly professional and managerial. Four lived on their own: three had been bereaved some time ago, and one was single. All had been, or were, regular churchgoers. They were chosen as likely to have personal experience of prayer.

Though in no way representative of the population at large, they do constitute a cross-section of the congregation of a suburban Anglican parish church, in the sixty to eighty-five age group.

The picture of prayer that emerged was one of conversation and communication, central to which was adoration of God and being quiet and relaxed in his presence. Most had a strong sense of the immediacy of God being with them, especially when they were in pain. Although God could be experienced as a 'nagging presence', there was little sense of the numinous as in any way threatening or judgemental. In their intercessionary prayer, there was some general reference to community issues, but most of their prayers were confined to family and personal matters. All prayed on their own, usually at a fixed time in the morning and evening, but prayer was generally seen as a spilling-over into the rest of life, and not restricted to one area or time. Their prayer seemed to be adaptive, and a meaning-making device for confrontation with changing, diminishing social roles and the ever-increasing certainty of death.

As prayer became more effective, more spontaneous and less formal, there grew an image of God as immanent in all his creation, and therefore personally available at any time.

Keyes emphasizes that older people need the support of familiar symbols and rituals, especially as their memory begins to fade and their concentration lapses. Through such rites as communion being brought to their homes, they can use role models — or living symbols — of those perceived to be in contact with the Holy.

There was general agreement among these six people that expectations of the elderly as 'a powerhouse of prayer' were quite unreasonable. Keyes remarks that:

> in old age, there is a tendency to become introspective, and therefore a real danger in seeing the elderly as a prayer powerhouse for the Church. It would be the exception, not the rule, to find someone in old age who could be such. Prayer becomes harder, not easier, as you age. Only if the seeds of an affective prayer life are sown early, will it flower in old age. . . . Prayer is like being in love, words become less necessary. Attitudes to prayer don't alter much as you age — nor does your self-image.[10]

The social function of this misconceived expectation might be the hope that the elderly can be usefully employed earning something akin to karma for those active in the world, like an extensive contemplative order. This could be seen as yet another example of ageism, a marginalizing of the elderly and projection on to them of a skill in handling the sacred — a skill that the old themselves do not feel that they possess.

It has been suggested that religious faith plays an increasingly important role in the life of older people, and that it is in old age that they return to the Church. Unfortunately, conclusive evidence of a correlation between religious faith, practice and church attendance is contradictory. Some thirty years ago Paul Maves, in 'Ageing, Religion and the Church', summarized a number of research studies on the religious behaviour of older people. He concluded that it would be more accurate to say that those who are now over sixty are somewhat more religious than those who are younger, but it is not clear that this is entirely related to ageing. Other studies suggest that many people carry out the same religious commitments that they acquired during their middle years.[11]

Robert Havinghurst, however, writing in 1972, points to an increased spiritual capacity in older people: 'In the spiritual sphere, there is perhaps no necessary shrinking of the boundaries, and perhaps there is even a widening of them.'[12]

A retired archbishop remarked, 'As I grow older, I discover I need to believe fewer things but each more deeply.' Similarly, a seventy-year-old layman has this to say: 'Having seen and experienced so much through a long life, one has an ability to filter out the non-essentials, and the peripheral commentary of life, thus achieving a sharper focus and truer perspective on meaningful issues. Perhaps it is best summed up in the phrase, "We wouldn't have to go through growth's phases if we had been born mature."'

Of the six in Keyes' study, a busy, retired schoolteacher described her prayer life as having a structure and pattern: 'A time, quiet time is set aside before breakfast. I read a Bible passage, a devotional book and talk to God. Before going to sleep, in bed I pray; at least I commit myself to God. For me, corporate worship in church can be mere words and no prayer at all; especially familiar words tend to flow over me. Set prayers are never too helpful — my mind is often elsewhere; but then thoughts that come along could be seen as answers to prayer.'[13]

But what of the spirituality of those who regularly attend OAP clubs, organized by churches or held on church premises? Do the programmes laid on by those in charge concentrate too much on filling in time for the members with bingo, craftwork, talks and 'bring-and-buy' sales? Are there opportunities at all for addressing spiritual needs?

Rabbi Julia Neuberger, in a talk given to the Age Concern National Conference in 1989, suggested that older people, especially widows, go to a place of worship primarily for a sense of community. There they find a place where they can belong, and there they receive pastoral care and attention that is not available elsewhere. Rabbi Neuberger affirms the contribution that religious institutions offer through well-laid-on social events, luncheon clubs and 'bright hours'. These may be a way-in to an ambiance where people can pray, and where other needs are met, particularly in times of bereavement.

Dorothy Jerome, of the Extension Studies Department of Sussex University, suggests in her writings that old people's clubs, especially those run by churches, provide a supportive setting where the members can together confront the issues of life and death and the continuity between past, present and future. In the club's warm, welcoming, communal atmosphere, the recently bereaved find themselves in good company. They are enabled to help one another to accept the new roles of widow or orphan. Standards of acceptable behaviour are set, and expressions of grief encouraged. The widow who makes no attempt is an object of disapproval. Some of us may find this surprising, yet the aim is to put death in the context of ongoing relationships. Sometimes the friendship of other survivors becomes more significant than what is on offer from kith and kin.

In this shared communality of experience, the way that God is present in every person's life is highlighted. Getting to understand each individual's story, with its joys and sorrows, helps all the members to see how God has been, and is, at work in our lives.

Prayer, as we have already said, does not get easier for the old. In Chapter 6, we quoted the admission from an elderly nun who found she could no longer concentrate or stay in one position, but she was also aware that God did not ask of her more than she could give.

We have mentioned the sharing of spiritual experience as immensely helpful to some. But others are too reticent and want to keep what goes on between themselves and God very private.

We both remember one old lady, who lived to be ninety-seven. She had been a regular churchgoer throughout her life and was able, in her late years, to adapt with ease and a sense of adventure to many of the changes in church attitudes during the middle of this century. Extemporary prayer in house groups would never have been much to her liking, but she found herself able to join a meeting for silent prayer once a week in her own home. This group and its members grew in importance to her when regular church attendance became difficult. She wanted a congregation of fellow-worshippers, yet one got the impression that her own praying was becoming increasingly inward and wordless. She would be silent for long periods and one could never be sure if one was interrupting prayer or sleep. Perhaps she did not have to stay wide-awake, but merely open to God, so that her prayer and his were one and the same.

Notes

1. C. G. Jung, *Memories, Dreams and Reflections*, Collins/Routledge 1963, p. 65.
2. ibid., p. 73.
3. T. S. Eliot, *Four Quartets*, Faber 1979.
4. E. Clark, *Workshop on Spiritual Needs*, St Mary's Bay and New Romney Discussion Paper 1988.
5. P. Tournier, *Learning to Grow Old*, SCM 1971, p. 240.
6. C. G. Jung, quoted in R. Wilhelm, *Secret of the Golden Flower: Chinese Book of Life*, Routledge 1962.
7. P. Teilhard de Chardin, *Le Milieu Divin*, Collins 1961, p. 81.
8. Jung, *Memories, Dreams and Reflections*.
9. ibid.
10. G. Keyes, 'Prayer, Spirituality and Ageing', in *Plus: quarterly journal of the Christian Council of Ageing*, September 1991, pp. 11–15.
11. P. Maves, 'Ageing, Religion and the Church', *Handbook of Social Gerontology*, Chicago University Press 1960.
12. R. Havinhurst, *Developmental Tasks and Education*, McKay 1972, p. 92.
13. G. Keyes, 'Prayer in Later Life', in *Plus: quarterly journal of the Christian Council of Ageing*, June 1991.

Glossary of Psychological Terms

Anima and animus	Unconscious contrasexual elements in the psyche of men (*anima*) and women (*animus*) (JUNG)
Archetype	Inherited part of the psyche that is linked to instinct. A hypothetical entity, manifesting itself through images (JUNG)
Counselling	Short-term therapeutic help, chiefly of an 'enabling' nature, that involves listening, attending and responding, usually in one-to-one weekly sessions
Ego	Personality viewed impersonally as structure, rather than definition of experiencing subject, or self (FREUD) (ego and self often used synonymously) *or* The centre of consciousness and mediator between conscious and unconscious. It is responsive to the demands of something superior, i.e. 'Self' (JUNG)
Image	That which can be perceived of the archetype — through dream, myth and metaphor. Expression of unconscious contents (JUNG)
Individuation	A life-long discovery of self — both as a unique human being and as part of a greater whole (JUNG)
Internalization	Process of taking in and owning aspects (things or people) from the external world. Often synonymous with introjection (opposite of projection)

Libido	Life force. Originally used by Freud to refer to sexual energy, but widened by Jung to include biological, psychological and spiritual energy
Narcissism	Derived from the story of Narcissus who fell in love with his own reflection. Used by Freudians, mostly in a pathological sense, as a result of parental deprivation — a failure to develop authentic self-love out of love for others. Jung, while agreeing to pathological usage, saw it as healthy and necessary for creativity
Projection	The external location of unacceptable aspects of the personality
Psyche	Jung's definition: 'Totality of all psychic processes, conscious as well as unconscious'
Psychoanalysis	Treatment of neurosis invented by Freud and elaborated by his followers. Strictly speaking, it is confined to members of the Institute of Psychoanalysis. Jung broke from Freud and introduced new concepts, notably 'individuation'. Jungian practitioners were originally known as 'analytical psychologists'
Psychodynamic	Describes an understanding of mental and emotional problems, which concentrates on internal workings of the mind and the relationship between parts of the 'self'
Regression	A backward movement to an earlier developmental stage, from which a new beginning may ensue
Self	'Not only the centre but also the whole circumference which embraces both conscious and unconscious; it is the centre of this totality, just as the ego is the centre of the conscious mind' (JUNG)
Shadow	Part of the personality that may be rejected, disowned or projected on to

	someone else. Often carries creative potential
Transference	Process by which feelings deriving from important (probably parental) figures in a person's past are displaced on to a psychotherapist or analyst. This is an important aspect of a therapeutic relationship, through which childhood conflicts can be reworked and given a chance of resolution
Unconscious	PERSONAL — Repository for all repressed personal experience (FREUD) COLLECTIVE — Repository of man's psychic heritage, universal as distinct from individual, though personal unconscious also acknowledged (JUNG)

Further Reading

Old age and death

de Beauvoir, S., *Old Age*, Penguin 1977.
de Beauvoir, S., *A Very Easy Death*, Penguin 1969.
Gilleard, C. J., *Living with Dementia*, Croom Helm 1984.
Hinton, J., *Dying*, Penguin 1967.
Israel, M., *Living Alone: The Inward Journey to Fellowship*, SPCK 1982.
Kroll, U., *Growing Older*, Collins 1988.
Kübler-Ross, E., *On Death and Dying*, Tavistock 1970.
Luke, H., *Old Age*, New York, Parabola Books 1987.
Nemiroff, R., and Colarusso, C., *The Race against Time: Psychotherapy and Psychoanalysis in the Second Half of Life*, New York and London, Plenum Press 1985.
Speck, P., and Ainsworth-Smith, I., *Letting Go: Caring for the Dying and Bereaved*, SPCK 1982.
Tournier, P., *Learning to Grow Old*, SCM 1971.

Pastoral care

Clebch, W., and Jaekle, C., *Pastoral Care in Historical Perspective*, New York, Harper Torchbacks 1967.
Forder, C., *The Parish Priest at Work*, SPCK 1947.
Foskett, J., and Lyall, D., *Helping the Helpers: Supervision and Pastoral Care*, SPCK 1988.
Jacobs, M., *Still Small Voice: An Introduction to Counselling*, SPCK 1982.

Jung (counselling and psychotherapy)

Fordham, M., *Jungian Psychotherapy*, John Wiley & Sons 1978.

Gordon, R., *Dying and Creating, A Search for Meaning*, Library of Analytical Psychology, vol. 4, 1978.

Jung, C. G., *Memories, Dreams and Reflections*, Collins/Routledge 1963.

Jung, C. G. (ed. Storr, A.), *Selected Writings*, Fontana 1983.

Lambert, K., *Analysis, Repair and Individuation*, Academic Press 1981.

Perry, C., *Listen to the Voice Within: A Jungian Approach to Pastoral Care*, SPCK 1991.

Redfearn, J. W. T., *My Self, My Many Selves*, Academic Press 1985.

Index

Index